Bearing the Saint

A Novel

Bearing the Saint

Donna Farley

CONCILIAR PRESS ✝ CHESTERTON, INDIANA

Bearing the Saint © 2010 Donna Farley

Published by   Conciliar Press
P.O. Box 748
Chesterton, IN 46304

Printed in the United States of America

ISBN 10: 1-936270-04-8
ISBN 13: 978-1-936270-04-0

Cover art and maps by Sarah Marina
(www.sarah-marina.com)

For LAWRENCE
my fellow pilgrim

acknowledgements

Thank You
Ic thancie eow

IN A WORK OF THIS KIND, THE WRITER WOULD PRODUCE a much poorer result without the aid of numerous other folk, and I therefore wish to express my gratitude to the following:

First, to Jane G. Meyer, who got this project off the ground, and to Katherine Hyde, who has seen it through to a safe landing. Two wonderful editors with sharp eyes and wise spirits. I am also grateful to artist Sarah Marina, and to Carla Zell and all the other talented folk at Conciliar Press for their work in making the book a solid and beautiful reality.

My regular beta-readers, Bev Cooke and Linda Finlayson, gave invaluable feedback under time pressure on the finished manuscript, and I am thankful for their long and ongoing friendship and co-struggling as fellow writers in Christ.

All the clever members of the Orthodox Writers at Rockaway in 2008 and 2009, including Katherine Hyde and my husband

Lawrence, helped me shape the book with their responses to chapter readings at earlier stages of the story.

I had special help in the kindness of strangers, too many to name, via several internet gathering places. In particular I want to thank Susan Hall at AbsoluteWrite for help with the storm scene. For a number of historical and linguistic details, I am indebted to several members of Tha Engliscan Gesithas, Norse Course, and Norsefolk re-enactment and discussion groups at YahooGroups. Any errors that turn up in the book are most certainly mine and not theirs.

As always, I thank my family for putting up with the inconveniences caused by the writing process.

The work put into this modest little story by me and these many other people can never compare in any way to the making, decorating, and translating of the Lindisfarne Gospels, but nevertheless I will dare to borrow the colophon added by the monk Aldred to that wondrous work:

For God and For Saint Cuthbert

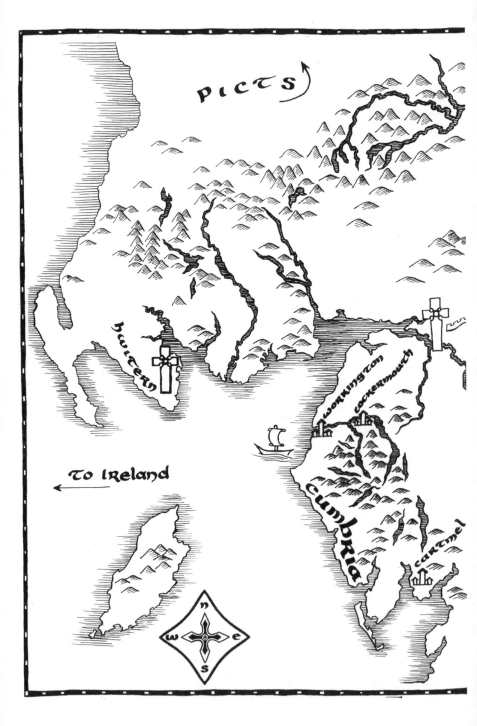

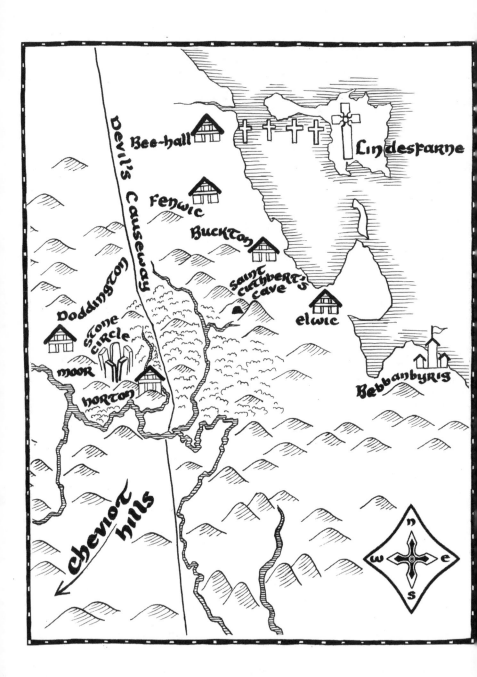

Part 1

Lindesfarne

A.D. 875

chapter one

"**I** HATE HAVING A BROTHER WHO WANTS TO BE A SAINT!" Edmund flung the words like spears before him as he burst in through the door of the hut.

Into the smoldering peat fire in the center of the hut he threw the broken wooden sword, the sword he had made only this morning from driftwood and a little hemp twine filched from his mother's store-box in the rafters. The sword his elder brother Hunred had just solemnly smashed against the rocks of Lindesfarne harbor, where the fishing nets were spread out to dry in the warm spring sun.

"He who lives by the sword shall perish by the sword," Hunred had said in his calm low voice, pale blue eyes fixed not upon Edmund but upon something not quite visible across the sparkling water to the southeast of the harbor . . . upon the Island of Farne. Hunred, Edmund knew, was thinking again of Saint Cuthbert, who had once lived as a hermit on that tiny isle.

And he's wishing Father hadn't been lost at sea last year, Edmund thought bitterly, *because if he hadn't been, Hunred would be tonsured a monk by now.* Instead, their mother Emma had begged the abbot and bishop to give her back her eldest son, to support his family by fishing. To be the man of the family.

Edmund didn't want to think about Father. So he had snatched up the broken pieces of his little play sword and fled his brother, pelting up the windy beach to the family hut. And now here he was inside with the sword fragments lying on the fire, and the only sound was the dispirited hiss of the flame from the peat, because his little sister Merewyn stood there with her mouth open but no sound coming out. Her distaff dangled and spun at the end of the length of yarn she held in the air. Her round blue eyes brimmed with tears.

Edmund turned this way and that, looking anywhere but at his sister. "Where's Mother?" he asked, gazing out the door as if he didn't already know.

Merewyn hesitated a moment before speaking. "Gone to trade fish for eggs," she said.

And then the hut darkened as Hunred's tall frame filled the doorway, the light making a sort of halo behind his chin-length hair, pale and straw-like. Edmund and Merewyn had the same hair, but Merewyn's was braided on each side, and Edmund's lay tied in a tail at the back of his neck. Hunred still wore his short, like the monastery schoolboys and novices, even though he had left the school over a year ago. Edmund's spine stiffened. He took a deep breath, but Hunred didn't even look at Edmund; instead he moved round the fire and past Merewyn. Edmund bit his lip almost to bloodletting as Hunred took a few twists of grass from the kindling box, laid them over the remnants of the driftwood sword, and cupped his hands to blow on the pitiful little flame struggling upward from the peat. The wood caught with a sudden orange flare and a crackle, and it seemed to Edmund that his own tongue too caught fire.

"Why did you have to do that?" he raged, hating the tears that he heard in his own voice. "You're supposed to be the man of the family now! Father would have tried my sword like a warrior when I showed it to him. You had no call to go breaking it, quoting at me like a monk when you aren't one!"

"Please stop!" Merewyn piped, but neither of the brothers heeded her. Hunred did not answer Edmund either. His pale eyes unfocusing, he straightened from his crouch by the fire. He held up his finger before his lips, a signal that Edmund had hated all the short time he spent at the monastery school when he was small.

"You can't make me be quiet like the schoolmaster, Hunred!"

But Hunred turned and left the hut. Growling, Edmund followed him out into the sunlight. Faintly from the church, above the sound of surf and the gulls mewing, came the urgent clattering of the monastery bell. Up and down the shore, the fisherfolk were coming out of their huts or pausing at their net mending.

Every day of his life, Edmund heard the bell at its work, but never had it clamored like this. Sometimes, the single booming toll that called the monks to matins would drift to the hut on the night wind, and Edmund would wake to a cold bed because Hunred had left their shared bunk to pray outside, still acting the monk. On great feasts, the bellmaster would make the bell sing like a lark in its wooden tower, and Edmund would find himself singing along, heart soaring. But now the frantic dinning of the bronze sent a thrill of fear along his spine.

"Go back in and watch the fire," said Hunred, still not looking at Edmund, and started southward along the shore toward the monastery.

Edmund threw his brother a curse that would have earned him a slap in the face from their mother. He sprinted ahead of Hunred, who never moved quickly, and dashed up the shore, sand and pebbles flying under his worn leather soles. If some news was afoot, Edmund should be there. He might be needed, because he was Bishop Eardwulf's fastest errand boy.

Turning inland, he ran up along the meadow lane to the cart-way that led to the monastery gate. And there in the way stood his friend Derwin, frowning as he listened to the bell, his pet raven Riddle perched on his shoulder. The jet-colored feathers made a match for Derwin's eyes and hair.

Riddle fluttered his wings and cried "Quork! Quork!" as Edmund slowed his approach. He felt the usual pang of envy at his friend's luck in rescuing and raising the bird, and the equally usual pang of guilt for envying his friend.

Derwin's head turned and he saw Edmund. "Edmund! I was on my way to see you, and then I heard the bell . . ."

Just then a black-maned chestnut mare came trotting out the monastery gate, bearing a young monk.

"Brother Herebert!" Edmund called.

The monk checked his mount with the reins. She snorted, clearly eager to be on the way. "No time to chat, Edmund," said Herebert. Edmund knew him well, for it was Herebert who had taught him and Derwin the messenger routes to the nearby mainland. He always had a cheerful word and a smile for everyone, but now an unfamiliar grimness masked his face. It made Edmund's stomach feel the way it did when the fishing boat dropped suddenly into a trough between waves. Herebert touched his heels to the mare's sides and made off past the mon-astery guesthouse toward the pilgrim way that crossed the sands to the mainland.

The boys watched him go, aghast. "But the tide is coming in already!" called Edmund. Lindesfarne was an island when the tide was high; when it was low, you could walk across, following the route marked by wooden crosses. But if you weren't careful, and the tide was coming in again, you could be caught too far from either the island or the mainland shore, cut off and betrayed by the currents, and even be drowned. Heart in mouth, he watched the horse jogging across the tidal flats; despite treacherous pebbles and threatening waves, she went on swiftly.

"He'll make it," said Derwin.

"Only because he and Frisk both know it so well." Edmund stared after the rider a moment more, then said, "Let's see what's so important that he's been sent out to race the tide!" He picked up his heels and dashed toward the gate.

Derwin too was one of the bishop's runners. After mass on feast days, the two friends liked to race from the lay church by the monastery wall to Derwin's home, the reeve hall, at the other end of the island. Edmund was nearly always faster.

Riddle launched himself into the air and flew on ahead, calling loudly as if to announce the race between the two. Along the rutted cartway they sped, Derwin at Edmund's heels. No one else had yet answered the summons of the bell, but a glance over Edmund's shoulder now showed men, women, and children hurrying along in the distance. Edmund put on a burst of speed; he liked to be first.

In through the open gate he ran, into the gravelly monastery grounds, and saw a pair of monks at the foot of the wooden bell tower by the church entrance. One tugged the rope back and forth, slamming the clapper against the bell as fast as Edmund's racing heart, again and again; without missing a beat, the second monk took over the rope while the first stood back, panting and shaking out his arms. A moment later, Derwin pulled up at Edmund's side, and the raven flew once more to his shoulder, where it sat screaming in time with the bell.

No one else was in sight in the open area amid the buildings of timber and thatch.

"What is it, what's happening?" Edmund shouted at the resting monk. The gonging of the bell swallowed his voice, but the monk caught Edmund's eye and pointed at the open double doors of the church.

Exchanging a frown with Derwin, Edmund went in, only belatedly crossing himself after passing over the threshold of the tall stone-and-timber church. Bishop Eardwulf stood, arms upraised before the altar and chanting, not one of the daily offices, but the service to Saint Cuthbert. A row of choir monks stood to each side of the bishop, responding to each petition, "Ora pro nobis!"

In the nave, the rest of the community's wool-habited monks knelt on the rush-strewn floor, the shaven crowns of their tonsures reflecting the light from the tall narrow windows, like great eggs in little nests.

While Edmund and Derwin stood there, other people began to file in behind them, so they moved out of the doorway and to the side, up near the stone tomb of Saint Cuthbert, beloved saint and patron of Lindesfarne. Riddle hopped off Derwin's shoulder and onto the tomb, but no one complained; Holy Cuthbert was famous for his love of birds and all God's creatures. Boys of twelve years' age, however, did not get quite as much tolerance, and a hard quick glance over the shoulder from his old schoolmaster sent Edmund to his knees, pulling Derwin down beside him.

"Do you think it's the Danes?" he whispered. His friend only looked at him, fright tensing all his features. Edmund didn't feel

fear, or not much. Not as much as excitement, and anger. . . .
"They took the monastery at Gyrwe last year," he reminded
Derwin. "Maybe the king is calling out churls as well as thegns
to fight now, even the farmers and fishers!"

"Or maybe he's made peace with the Danes," said Derwin,
but Edmund watched the monks in the choir on the other side
of the church. Except for their mouths moving in the plaintive
refrain, their pale faces were still as carved stone, their eyes distant with foreboding.

"It isn't peace," Edmund said.

"Quork! Quork!" boomed Riddle.

chapter two

AS THE BELL KEPT TOLLING, MORE OF THE FISHER-folk trickled in to stand near the back of the church. No farmers—the reeve hall was out of sound of the bell.

While the service flowed on, Edmund mouthed the refrain, *Ora pro nobis*. His mind, however, raced back and forth through time. It had to be the Danes attacking. The monks of Gyrwe at the mouth of the River Tyne, only a few days' sail down the coast, had dispersed last autumn, fleeing the Northmen's ships in terror. The Danes loved to raid the undefended monasteries of the Angle and Saxon kingdoms, seizing the golden treasures made to beautify the church, and capturing slaves to sell in far-off lands. This time, though, the Danish chief Halfdan and all his warriors, instead of taking their loot and sailing off again, had settled down and spent the winter by the Tyne.

Edmund wished he could see the bishop's expression, but from this angle only the side of his clean-shaven face was visible above the embroidered collar of his vestments. Edmund noticed a strange monk standing by the wall, a little back from the north choir. With curly tonsure gray as iron and skin like leather, the short but sturdy-looking man had the bearing of an outdoorsman. And yet . . . he also had a faraway look in his eyes that reminded Edmund of Hunred. Edmund glanced away and back at the bishop.

Bishop Eardwulf knew everything. He gathered things with those sharp gray eyes of his, turning them over in his mind and weaving them together till they all came out right, like a fisherman making a net. And what he didn't see with his own eyes, messengers brought to him from near and far. This time the news came from this visiting monk, Edmund was sure of it.

Before Father was lost at sea, Edmund had spent a little time at the monastery school, as all the boys of Lindesfarne did. The silence didn't suit him, and the schoolmaster got tired of having to beat Edmund's palms with a willow switch day after day for talking in class. And the writing, and the *reading* . . . the tracks of gulls and dogs and cats and people across the sand made sense to Edmund. But it seemed to him that the black strokes made by quill and ink marched across the vellum pages in the schoolroom, baffling and unconquerable as . . . well, as a band of Danish warriors.

One particularly bad school day, Edmund's tongue had earned him not only a palm-switching but a spell of exile, standing still and silent outside the school hall. Brother Trumwin had, however, neglected to order him to face the wall, so Edmund was able to stave off boredom by watching the habited monks going about the yard on their silent errands. When a lull fell in the monastery's quiet bustle, a lanky rust-colored cat strutted into the center of the empty yard, sat down, and began to wash its face.

It wasn't *talking* just to cluck your tongue at a cat, was it? And it wasn't *moving*—not moving away from the spot where you'd been told to stand, at least—to reach out your hand to the cat, rubbing the fingers together till the creature stopped grooming itself and stared at your hand. . . .

The cat got up and paced over to Edmund, unhurried and pretending only vague interest, till it came a few paces from him and stopped. Edmund had to bend down and stretch to reach the animal.

Between one breath and the next, the cat's front paw lashed out, scoring Edmund's forearm from elbow to wrist. A shriek burst from Edmund, and the cat dashed away toward the gate. Edmund's feet came unstuck from their spot and he streaked after the cat. "You dirty devil cat! I'll teach you!"

The cat suddenly jogged aside and ran lickety-split in through the just-opened door of the church—in past the wool-cassocked legs of Bishop Eardwulf as he emerged.

The bishop's right eyebrow rose. "Edmund son of Tida," he said. Not a shout, not a scold, just his name.

Edmund swallowed. "I'm sorry, Holy Father! I—I was standing—the cat just—well, I clucked to her and waggled my fingers, but I wasn't calling or talking, I wasn't!"

"You had best take that arm over to the infirmary for cleaning," said the bishop. "Cat scratches can fester."

Edmund glanced at the freely bleeding gash on his arm. It did smart, but not as much as the inner wound. That cat had looked like a friend to Edmund, and the sudden betrayal had lit a surprising fury in him. "Yes, my lord bishop, but Brother Trumwin told me to stand by the wall—"

"Never mind," said the bishop. "I want you to run to the infirmary. Now, as fast as you can!"

Edmund stared.

"Now! Fast!"

"Yes, my lord bishop!" Edmund spun on his heel and pelted through the yard, back past the school hall, round the corner of the cook house and refectory, away past the schoolboys' and novices' dormitories and the monks' little cell huts, till he skidded to a stop inside the open door of the infirmary. The leech-monk, Brother Ninian, looked up in alarm from the table where he sat tying herbs into bunches. Edmund tumbled out his tale while the elderly monk frowned in annoyance.

"A cat scratch? That's it?" He shook his head and told Edmund to sit down while he fetched hot water from the iron pot he kept constantly on the boil over the steady hearth fire in the center of the room. Edmund sat on the bench biting his lip for a few minutes till the door darkened and Bishop Eardwulf came in.

"That was fast running, Edmund," said the bishop. "Did it make you out of breath?"

"Oh no. It wasn't far."

Brother Ninian took hold of his injured arm and dabbed at it with clean linen and water from the pot. It was so hot Edmund gave a little gasp, but the leech-monk continued patting.

"You can run a long way, then. Fast," the bishop continued.

"Oh yes. I run with Derwin and sometimes some other boys, all the way from the lay church to the reeve hall every feast day after mass. Even if it's raining. But not if it's snowing—then we make snowballs and have a battle instead." Edmund suddenly felt his cheeks flame—he had said too much, as usual. The bishop's eyes narrowed shrewdly, but Edmund thought his mouth looked like it was smiling. He hoped.

Brother Ninian tied up the ends of a linen bandage around

his arm. Edmund thanked him and said, "I must run back to my lessons now."

"Oh, no, Edmund son of Tida," said the bishop. Definitely smiling now, but Edmund wasn't sure that was good. "I have told your schoolmaster you will be serving a different punishment today."

Edmund's mouth went dry. Still, he knew what to say: "I will obey humbly, my lord bishop!"

Edmund wished Bishop Eardwulf wouldn't look like he was trying to keep from laughing while he said to the leech-monk, "Light a marked candle, Brother." To Edmund he said, "Now you run to the reeve hall, touch the doorpost, and run back here. We shall see how much candle is left."

"Yes, my lord bishop!" Edmund turned and dashed out the door. Five steps later he remembered to turn around, duck back in, snatch the bishop's right hand to kiss his ring and run back out again.

He pelted back to the monastery gate, almost tripping on the rust-colored cat as he passed the church. Out through the gate, past the guest house. Passing the pilgrim way on his left, where plovers and godwits picked about as the running tide pooled over the sands.

As he passed the layfolks' church and burial ground on his right, a sparrow hawk shrieked overhead, and a mouse skittered across his path. But he did not break stride, continuing on through the meadow, grass and heath and creeping willow slapping at his bare legs as he went. Not stopping even when he stepped in sheep droppings. *Run, run, run—no, wait!* He slowed a moment, then breathed, counting to five. He had to run to the reeve hall and back, he had to save something for the way *back*! How he wished he had Derwin to pace him—but Derwin was still imprisoned with the other boys in the school. Edmund hadn't wanted to boast to the bishop, but he knew he was the fastest of the boys by far. Only Derwin came close.

He started off again, just a little slower. Still, he did not stop even when Derwin's elder sister Aelfleda called to him from the field where she was gathering herbs in a basket. The hall with its sloped thatched roof loomed larger now, and he dreaded the bustle about its open front yard, dogs scuffling and children wailing, women carrying water and old men sitting in the sun over a game of *taefl*. Gritting his teeth, he flew past them all, slapped his hand against the oaken doorpost so hard it stung, and turned to flee the chorus of surprise. Yapping dogs followed in his wake, till someone whistled them back.

He ran faster now. You could think when you ran, but it slowed you down, so he wouldn't think. He just pictured himself leaping in over the threshold of the infirmary. *Don't think about the candle!* he told himself, but it was too late. Now he was thinking of the yellow beeswax, the honeyed scent and the dreamy steady flame, burning relentlessly down toward the next quarter-hour mark.

"Agh! No thinking!" he yelled out loud, startling a thrush from a hawthorn thicket as he passed. Just then the monastery bell began to toll for the noon meal. He pumped his legs harder and burst in through the gate. The yard swarmed with monks and novices and schoolboys, all on their way to the refectory.

"Look out!" he shouted, and ducked between Schoolmaster Trumwin and another monk. He swerved past a cluster of monks emerging from the scriptorium, only to be met by his startled schoolfellows. "Make way!"

Derwin stepped aside for him at once, but little Cuthwin

the smith's boy was too slow. Down he went, howling, and Edmund's race ended.

"Cuthie! I'm sorry, I'm sorry—are you hurt bad?"

"What are you about, Edmund?" Brother Trumwin's wrath descended like a storm breaker on the shore.

"I'm sorry!"

"Please, Schoolmaster," said Derwin, "May Edmund and I have leave to take Cuthie to the infirmary?"

Cuthwin was sniffling, his face bloody and dusty. Brother Trumwin growled, then nodded. "Well?" he said to the rest of the boys who were bunched about. "What are you minnows staring at?"

They scampered away, and Edmund and Derwin took the smaller boy toward the infirmary, meeting Brother Ninian on the way as he shuffled toward the refectory. The leech-monk clucked his tongue at Cuthwin's injuries and took him under his wing back to the infirmary.

"What's going on, Edmund?" Derwin asked.

"Tell you later. You go eat," said Edmund, and paced glumly after the leech-monk. No point hurrying now.

But while he was dragging his feet, Bishop Eardwulf stepped out of the infirmary.

"Edmund! In through that door!"

"Yes, my lord bishop!" Edmund gasped and darted ahead, but this time looked where he was going. Cuthwin sat on the bench. Brother Ninian, seeing Edmund inside the door, wetted his thumb and forefinger and reached over to pinch out the flame of the marked candle with a little hiss. Edmund stared in confusion; had he been fast enough? And—fast enough for what?

Bishop Eardwulf cleared his throat in the doorway behind him, and Edmund leapt out of the way. "Edmund son of Tida."

"Yes, my lord bishop!"

"Always *finish the race*, Edmund. Do you understand?"

The bishop's gaze seemed to go right into Edmund. Like a stylus into a wax practice tablet, graving the words deep and clear. "Yes, my lord bishop. Always finish the race."

From that day, Edmund had been let out of school and back to the fishing with his father—on condition that when he was ashore, he would serve as messenger whenever the bishop called. Brother Herebert, chief among the monks and novices who did the same task, brought him along to learn the way to places on the nearby mainland; soon Edmund could go alone at need, sometimes by boat if the crossing was under the tide. It was exciting to visit the halls of important folk, and be treated with deference because he brought word from Bishop Eardwulf— bishop of the whole of the north! There was even a day when Edmund was brought along with the bishop's retinue to King Ricsige's fortified hall at Bebbanbyrig itself . . .

With a start Edmund rose out of his memories, like a man breaking the surface of the sea after a deep dive. The lapping waves of the refrain, *Ora pro nobis*, had turned to a sudden and echoing *Amen*. Edmund's legs tingled as he struggled to his feet along with Derwin and all the assembled folk.

Bishop Eardwulf turned toward them, and the silence grew thick as he surveyed the crowd. Edmund had never seen his face so pale.

"My brethren," he said at last. "My children in God. The monks of Saint Cuthbert must leave Lindesfarne."

chapter three

AYFOLK GASPED ALOUD, WHILE MONKS CROSSED themselves, murmuring *"Miserere!"* Riddle hackled on Derwin's shoulder, crying out in his hoarse raven voice. Derwin smoothed his feathers, hushing him.

The bishop held up his hands for the gathering to quieten, and his gaze fell on Edmund. "Edmund son of Tida."

Cheeks burning as heads turned curiously toward him, Edmund cleared his throat. "Yes, my lord bishop."

"Run to the reeve hall. Stitheard the reeve must meet with us at once." He looked out over the heads of the monks, at the lay people crowded in by the door. "And everyone else on this island who is not bound to a sickbed."

"Yes, my lord bishop!"

Edmund ran out. His mind raced along with his feet. He had not even looked at Derwin as he left. Stitheard the reeve was Derwin's own father, and Derwin could have been the one chosen for this errand; but they both knew Edmund was faster.

Edmund's legs, a little longer now than they had been that

first time the bishop made him run the length of the island and back, carried him ever faster toward the reeve hall. He arrived panting and startled the hall folk in the yard by yelling out, "Reeve Stitheard! News!"

Derwin's sister Aelfleda, limping on the crooked leg she had been born with, came to bring him water, which he gulped gratefully. Her father emerged into the sunny yard, the rest of the hall's inhabitants at his back.

Reeve Stitheard, tall and broad, proudly bore the same raven hair as his son Derwin; but unlike Derwin's schoolboy cut, Stitheard's hung in long braids over his shoulders, twined with beads of jet and glass and even amber. He looked like a warrior, and indeed Edmund knew he owned a sword and spear and shield, for all he was in fact a farmer. Like all of Lindesfarne, Stitheard was bound to the bishop, and the lands he worked belonged to the monastery. But as reeve, the chief man on the island outside the monastery, he held the rank of *thegn*, equal with the warrior-men who owned lands of their own and who served the king of Northumbria. No one really expected Stitheard or any of the bishop's men to fight, but he had learned how and taught Derwin a little. Derwin would have preferred to play with Riddle, but Edmund had been thrilled when they allowed him to join their practice once or twice.

Edmund quivered—would the fighting come even to Lindesfarne?

"Well?" the reeve said gruffly.

When Edmund spilled out the frightening summons, Stitheard barked at his followers to spread the word and come as they could or would. Edmund turned back toward the monastery, his itch to know more goading him along quickly. When he entered the monastery gate, he found people milling about the

wide yard before the church. The monks had brought out one
of the long dining tables from the hall and placed the bishop's
cathedra atop it. Edmund's mouth fell open as he saw its gilding
glint in the sunlight. *The Danes—if they come here, they'll steal
that! A holy thing from God's church—take it away on their dragon-
ships to be some wicked murderous raider chieftain's throne . . .*

Finish the race! he reminded himself. He found the bishop's
secretary setting up a writing desk beside the table with the
cathedra on it, and told him the reeve and hall folk would soon
be there. Then, after a drink at the well, he found Derwin and
the other schoolboys. They were playing with stones in the dust,
building a model fort. Edmund thought, *Lindesfarne doesn't have
a fort.* "We ought to play at swords instead!" he burst out.

"You know we aren't allowed to have a fight on the monastery
grounds, Edmund—not even a play-fight," Derwin said. With
Derwin, it was always peace and reason.

"The reeve and hall folk are here!" went up a shout from the
gate. A brother rang the bell three times, and the crowd fell
silent. Some young monks helped the bishop up to his cathedra,
where all the people could see and hear him. A stool was set at
his right hand, and the unfamiliar monk Edmund had noted in
the church took his place there.

People made way for Stitheard, who came to the front. He
did not wait to be addressed. "My lord bishop, you summoned
me," he said, ducking his head as he kissed the bishop's ring.
"What is this about the monks leaving?"

Edmund had always admired the reeve's boldness, but this
was the first time he had seen the bishop show a flicker of annoyance at it. The people began to murmur, and the bishop rose
from his seat.

When they fell quiet again, he said, "My wisdom has failed.

I thank God for our brother Abbot Eadred of Luel. He crossed the pilgrim way yesterday to take counsel with us, and this morning he told me he had heard the voice of Saint Cuthbert in the night."

People gasped and crossed themselves. Some fell to their knees, whispering "*miserere*" or "*Deo gloria!*" Edmund chanced to glimpse his brother standing with his friend, the red-haired Franco, who was among the novices. Hunred had gone pale, but his eyes had a strange light in them.

Stitheard spoke again, his voice hard. "And does our saint tell us to abandon him? God be my witness, though all the monks on this island should flee like mice, I tell you that of all the lay-folk not one man, woman, or child, fisher, farmer, or craftsman, will ever leave our saint!"

The voice of the people rose in distress—and to Edmund's surprise, Hunred shouldered himself forward to Stitheard's side and flung himself at the bishop's feet with a wail.

"My lord bishop, we will not leave Holy Cuthbert! We cannot!"

The bishop held up a hand for quiet again. "But we will not leave him. Abbot Eadred recalled the words of Saint Cuthbert himself, written down by the Wise Bede of Gyrwe: 'If you are forced to choose between two evils, I would rather you left the island, taking my bones with you.'"

This time the crowd was truly stunned. Yet the reeve took only a moment to recover. "No! Bishop though you be—Cuthbert is *our* saint too!"

"You cannot leave us! You cannot take our saint!" cried an old fisherman, and some of the littler children began to wail.

The next voice that rose above the din was that of Aelfleda, as daring as her father the reeve, speaking from the back of the little donkey she rode to spare her leg. "O father bishop, who will protect us, if you take our saint away? Who will feed us, as he fed the boy with the fish brought by the eagle? Who will heal us, as his relics have healed even some who are with us today?"

People began to shout out how they or their loved ones had received healing. Edmund, and all the other children on the island, when they gathered at the reeve hall on high feasts, always loved to hear Aelfleda's stories, most of them about Saint Cuthbert.

"Cuthbert help us!" cried Hunred, and suddenly Edmund found himself caught up with the tide of voices crying, "Cuthbert! Cuthbert and God!"

Were those tears Edmund saw in the bishop's eyes as he held up his hands for quiet again? "My children! My dear ones!" It took a few moments before they would hear, and a few more before he could speak. "The Danes will loot our church, perhaps burn it, and take any treasures we cannot carry with us. You must all seek refuge on the mainland—"

"NO!" shouted Stitheard. "I say it again—where Cuthbert goes, there go the *haliwerfolc*, the people of the saint! And that is the folk of Lindesfarne, monk and lay, old and young, fisher and farmer!"

Edmund's jaw dropped. Even Stitheard wanted to flee, and not fight? Though Derwin pulled at his sleeve in warning, words burst from Edmund's lips. "But won't the king call us *all* to fight? Why do we flee?"

"No, my boy, King Ricsige won't fight," said Stitheard, and his tone was bitter. "Don't you know it's the Danes that put him on the throne? The Danes come this time for more than loot. They want land. Half Northumbria's fighting men are years dead now. We cannot win."

People's eyes turned to Bishop Eardwulf, who sighed, his brow furrowed. "You speak truth, Stitheard. Northumbria is justly punished by these attacks, for our impiety and careless living, for the oppression of the poor, and the years of fighting and murder amongst our own leaders. No, I tell you, we will follow the word of Abbot Eadred. And—bless you all," he said, scanning the crowd, "If you will not seek refuge on the mainland, then you choose to tread a path of great trial and danger with us."

"And with Saint Cuthbert!" said Aelfleda.

The bishop smiled a real smile at last. "Yes, with our saint, the gift of God Almighty to us and to all Northumbria!"

Cheers went up of "Cuthbert!" and *Gloria Dei!*

"My lord bishop," said Stitheard. "I will bring our best cart and my ox Lindo to bear our holy saint, and choose six men to tend the cart and guard its holy burden."

There was the reeve's boldness again, thought Edmund, and there was the bishop's hint of irritation too.

"I thank you, Stitheard, for the provision of cart and ox. But the attendants—" Bishop Eardwulf looked out at the layfolk, and then back at the clump of monks in their undyed habits.

A sudden tension hung in the air, like a storm about to break, and Edmund felt he could almost see the bishop change course. "There will be *seven* attendants, for seven is a holy number. Four of them will be monks of my choosing, three of them laymen chosen by the reeve."

Stitheard made a low dissatisfied grumble. Edmund saw the prophetic monk Eadred lean over and speak in the bishop's ear. One corner of the bishop's mouth turned up. "*Three* monks, I will choose. And one novice."

A cheer went up. Riddle launched from Derwin's shoulder and took suddenly to the air, circling over the heads of the bishop and Abbot Eadred. Edmund gasped, and other people began to point and exclaim, "An omen!"

The bishop too looked up, and as he did, the raven flew off over the gate, in the direction of the pilgrim way. The bishop crossed himself, and the people did too. "We will gather at the monastery gate tomorrow at dawn, ready to make the crossing at low tide. Go now with God's blessing," he said, and made the sign of the cross over them, lifting his hand high over the crowd as they bowed their heads.

"Did you see how cleverly the bishop and Eadred made peace with my father?" said Derwin. "A novice is neither full monk nor yet a layman any more! So the numbers are even!"

While the crowd was breaking up, talking excitedly and hurrying off to their homes, Hunred fastened himself to the reeve's side, hastening his usually slow-paced steps to keep up with Stitheard's long, quick strides.

"Look at my brother," said Edmund in disgust. "Wouldn't you know it, he thinks *he* should be one of the bearers!" He scuttled closer to hear what Hunred was saying. Aelfleda, brow wrinkled, came toward them on her donkey from the other direction, and behind her Edmund's mother and sister.

"Reeve, I beg you—" began Hunred.

"I told you, boy—"

"I am not a boy!" Hunred said, and planted himself in the reeve's path, forcing him to halt. Aelfleda's eyes went round, and she put one hand over her mouth.

"I have been the man of my family for over a year," Hunred declared, "and I have all the strength of one who pulls oars and raises sails and hauls nets!"

"Yes, so what do you know of cart and oxen?" Stitheard snapped.

"Father," Aelfleda put in, "we have you for oxherd. If we have one other from the hall folk, that leaves just one bearer from among the fisherfolk. Cuthbert is their saint as well."

Hunred closed his eyes and bent his head. Stitheard looked at his daughter from beneath stormy brows, but she did not flinch, gazing back at him hopefully.

"Very well, Hunred, son of Tida," growled the reeve, still frowning at his daring daughter. "Fetch your things and come to the hall at once."

"Thank you, reeve!" said Hunred, and ran for home, never a glance to spare for his mother or sister, or for Aelfleda, who had spoken for him and who sat by on her donkey, mouth half open to speak to him as he flew past.

chapter four

ITH HIS LOST FATHER'S PRIZED TIN LANTERN IN one hand, his fishing pike in the other, and a sack over his shoulder, Edmund picked his way along. He could see more lanterns and torches at the monastery gate, and a glimmer of light in the small windows of the church, from which could be faintly heard the chanting of the monks. The sky was growing paler, but not quickly enough for Edmund.

"Edmund! Slow down!" Merewyn tugged at his sleeve.

"Do, Edmund, we need the light too," his mother's tired voice said a few steps behind.

With a sigh Edmund complied. He had slept little, listening to the tide crawling up the beach, then beginning to recede again. It would be at its lowest within an hour or two now. *And then there's no turning back . . .*

At the gate a crowd was already gathered, murmuring together. A rooster in a cage crowed, and cartwheels creaked and groaned as more hall folk arrived. A dog began to whine, but stopped abruptly when its master snapped at it.

Handing the lantern off to his little sister, Edmund sought and found Derwin with Aelfleda among the crowd.

"Father and Raedwulf the cartwright and your brother have taken the oxcart in through the gate," said Aelfleda.

Riddle cawed in greeting and consented to let Edmund stroke his feathers.

"You brought fishing gear?" Derwin asked, looking at Edmund's pike with its barbed tip for spearing eels. A long-handled net peeked out the top of his sack, which also held Edmund's spare clothing, and some dried fish in a packet at the bottom.

"Just the pike, and this net, I hope they will do for river fishing … Derwin, we had to cut our big nets to pieces. So the wretched *Danes* couldn't use them. When I think of all the hours I spent tying those knots!"

"The shepherds are down by the pilgrim way already," said Derwin, "to drive the sheep across before we get there, the minute the tide clears. They're going to leave them at Bee-hall."

"Look," said Aelfleda. "The church."

The lights had been quenched, and the chanting ceased. The crowd shuffled, and Edmund stood tiptoe to see past the broad, pack-laden shoulders before him. A pair of novices bearing lanterns on poles came out through the gate, flanking another who led the way with a gilded cross mounted on a tall pole. Then came the bishop, all his church finery packed away somewhere and dressed as simply as his monks, stepping along in solemn time with the chant. Behind him, Stitheard led the cart-ox, named Lindesfarne after the holy island that was their home.

"That's it!" Derwin whispered. "The saint's coffin!"

People crossed themselves and knelt. Edmund gazed in awe at the wooden coffin. What a feat it must have been for the monks to open the stone lid of the tomb in the church and lift out the coffin . . . You didn't have to be a monk to love Cuthbert; he was everyone's saint. *Mine too*, thought Edmund.

Simple figures and old runes adorned the sides of the coffin, but Edmund could not make them out in the gray dawn and flickering torchlight. Attendants paced alongside the two-wheeled cart—two monks ahead of the wheels, then Hunred and Raedwulf behind them. Bringing up the rear, before the choir of monks, came a third monk and the one novice chosen to attend the coffin, who turned out to be Hunred's red-haired friend Franco.

The monks flooded past like a following tide in their undyed habits. Two of them closed the monastery gate behind them, and people rose to follow the procession.

"But who's going to guard us?" Edmund muttered to Derwin as they tramped onward with the procession to the pilgrim way. "Your father is practically the only trained fighter!"

"It's a holy task, bearing the saint," said Derwin. "You can't carry tools of bloodshed when you're bearing a saint. And Father says one or two weapons will be no use against a warband of Danes."

"So who has the weapons now?"

Derwin kept silent, and for the first time Edmund noticed the long wrapped bundle over Derwin's shoulder.

"*You* have your father's sword?"

Derwin shrugged. "A couple of the hall men have spears." He spoke reasonably, as always, but Edmund thought there was a little irritation in the way his friend looked at him. While the eastern light grew at their backs and frustration grew inside him, his grip on his lightweight fishing pike tightened. It would do as a weapon in a pinch. Maybe.

Yesterday while they packed, his mother had told him, "All

the fishermen will have to help feed us as we travel, Edmund. What help the farmfolk will be once their sacks of grain are gone, I don't know."

"They'll bring chickens for eggs, won't they? And cows for milk?"

"Surely they will. But the chickens and cows have to be fed too," she had pointed out.

The sun was up now, casting their long shadows before them. The company of the saint stood at the edge of the tidal sands between Lindesfarne and the mainland. On the far side they could see smoke curling up from the roofs of the little collection of huts at Fenham on the other side. Further north, to their right, the shepherds were already moving their bleating animals along the angled pathway, marked by wooden crosses, toward Bee-hall.

They started across, and at once the cart stuck in the wet sand. That was why the strong attendants were needed. Still, Edmund twitched at the slight delay, and suddenly he dashed up to the bishop.

"My lord bishop, please you, I would be glad to run over to Bee-hall and tell them we are coming!"

The bishop looked kindly at him. "Thank you, Edmund, but I sent Brother Herebert there yesterday on horseback. They will be ready for us. But no one need wait for the saint."

Edmund turned to Derwin. "Race?"

"On the sands? With all this?" Derwin said, shrugging his shoulders under his pack.

"We can at least go faster than all these!" said Edmund, prodding his friend to look behind at the old folk, little children, heavy-burdened men and women leading fractious goats or reluctant cows, or pushing high-laden hand-barrows.

"I can run!" Merewyn piped suddenly. Even she was carrying

a small pack. She ran on ahead of the longer-legged boys, and didn't turn back though her mother called to her.

Edmund smirked. "She doesn't know how to pace herself. She'll tire before we catch her. Come on!" Tucking the pike to his side, he sprinted ahead, leaving Derwin to join him.

It *was* tougher to run with the weight of the pack and the impediment of the long pike, but Edmund felt his way to the proper pace. Merewyn was streaking along despite the slippery eel-grass, sliding stones, and tide pools between her and the sheep, her light weight an advantage on this uncertain ground.

Derwin jogged up beside him. "Ed! She's headed up into the way there!"

The warning came too late—Edmund stepped up his speed, but Merewyn had pulled up beside the sheep and made to run on past them. One of the dogs snapped at her as if to herd her along with the animals. She shrieked, and some of the distracted sheep turned aside into her path.

"Stupid fisher child!" one of the shepherds yelled, and the others cursed at her, but still somehow she ended up amid the flock and began to wail in terror. Edmund dropped his pike and swooped in to snatch her up. As soon as the streams of bleating sheep had passed around them, he set her down and launched into a scolding torrent, keeping it up until Derwin strolled up carrying the pike. Aelfleda trotted behind him on the donkey.

"You might have been killed!" Edmund stormed.

"I'm sorry!" Merewyn sobbed.

"I'll take care of her, Edmund," said Aelfleda. Edmund gave his little sister one more glower, snatched the pike from Derwin and stalked quickly on, breathing hard.

"I suppose we shan't run and catch up to the sheep ourselves now," Derwin observed. Edmund heard amusement in his friend's voice but ignored it. Derwin knew him too well. Edmund was so angry with his little sister because he himself had been within a hairsbreadth of making the same mistake—he who was older and knew better.

"She might have been trampled if you hadn't scooped her up," Derwin consoled him.

"It should have been Hunred looking out for her. He's supposed to be the man of the family."

Derwin was good at saying nothing. Sometimes Edmund was glad of it, and sometimes he wasn't. This time he couldn't make up his mind which it was, so he changed the subject and talked the rest of the way to the mainland about where they would sleep and what they would get for dinner at Bee-hall.

They arrived at Bee-hall well before noon, and got no dinner, only well water and a little bread and hard cheese to take them on their way. The bishop frowned when some grumbled, and loudly thanked the hall-thegn for sharing Bee-hall's limited food stores with such a large company.

People were now milling about and trying to order themselves somehow before setting off again. The thegn of Bee-hall and his people bowed for the bishop's blessing in front of Saint Cuthbert's coffin. As the bishop turned to lead his procession once more, the tetchy old Lindesfarne shepherd who had scolded Merewyn hurried up and knelt before him.

"Please, my lord bishop," the man said. "I know they'll do their best here at Bee-hall to watch our flocks. But I can't leave the dogs, I can't. I can't bring them with the saint, what would they do with no sheep to herd? I must stay here." He cast his gaze downward, shame making his cheeks bright.

A silence fell on them all, Islanders and Bee-hall folk alike. Only some of the cows lowed, and caged chickens clucked distractedly. The bishop's eyes met those of Stitheard, who looked uncomfortable but said nothing. "So it begins. Stay with my blessing, then, shepherd. I hope I can care for my flock as well as you care for yours." He traced the cross over the shepherd, who kissed his ring.

Then the bishop looked around at the others. "I did not ask you all to bear the saint with us. Any who will go no further—I lay it upon this estate to take you in till places can be found on our other estates."

A woman sobbed, then made her way forward to kneel at the bishop's feet for a blessing. One by one, several other people followed—people Edmund had known from the time he could talk.

The procession set off on its way again, and though the spring sun shone brightly, it felt like a cloud was hovering over them. *Finish the race*, thought Edmund. But where was the end of this race going to be?

chapter five

HE SUN WAS GETTING WARM OVERHEAD ON THE road to Fenwic, the next estate to the south, but that didn't stop Edmund jogging out ahead of the coffin-bearing party. He left the awkward fishing pike with Derwin, who had declined to join him this time. Edmund knew the way well from frequent errands, and the way to the other estates nearby. Brother Herebert had already left Bee-hall and ridden ahead to Fenwic before the company arrived.

Edmund loped along past the outlying settlement of Fenham Hill, leaving the procession well behind him now. As he pressed on downslope toward Fenwic hall, he saw a figure coming up the road toward him. He squinted against the bright sun of the late morning.

Long-robed, but in brown and yellow, not in the plain habit of the monks; and yes, there was long hair or a veil on the head . . . it had to be a woman. A short woman or a girl, he realized as the figure quickened its pace.

He slowed almost to a stop and called out, *"Waes thu hal!"*

The girl ran panting up to him. Without bothering to return his greeting she said, "Is the bishop coming?"

"Yes. And all of Lindesfarne with him." Edmund supposed she couldn't help the snubbiness of her freckled nose, but it gave her an insolent look.

"I need to see him," she said.

She couldn't be any older than he was; she still went without a veil over her wispy hair, not as yellow as his own but not quite as coppery as the novice Franco's either.

"What about?"

Her eyes flashed, shrewd and sea-green. "What business is it of yours?" She made to head on up the hill past him, but he snagged her arm as she went and spun her back to face him.

"Edmund son of Tida is my name, and I am one of Bishop Eardwulf's messengers. If it's anything important, you'd better tell me so I can run to tell him."

"I can run perfectly well myself!" she said, but she didn't. She shook off his hand and started plodding up the slope, still breathing hard from her run.

"I'm used to running," said Edmund, tagging at her heels and trying to sound as reasonable as Derwin, though really he was quite put out by her rudeness. "I can get your message to the bishop quicker."

Still she made no reply and continued to toil determinedly up the hill—*finishing her race*, thought Edmund, *no matter how slow* . . . He tried again: "I've been to Fenwic a lot, but I don't remember seeing you. Are you new there?"

"Do you never stop talking, boy?"

The stinging remark, too true, stopped him in his tracks just as they topped the rise. The sound of chanting floated towards them, and a moment later the saint's procession came up over the far side of the hill. The girl picked up her skirts and once more broke into a run, falling down before the bishop's feet. The whole procession trundled to a halt. *And he's frowning at her*, Edmund thought with satisfaction.

"Child, what do you want?" said the bishop.

"My lord bishop, do you not remember me? My name is Caris. From Aelfsdene!"

"Ah! Yes. Now you are a free woman, serving us at our estate of Fenwic..."

"And you promised, Bishop Eardwulf! When I am old enough, either you would find me a husband, or place me in a monastery!"

"So I did, young Caris. I see you are not yet quite old enough, but now the Danes are attacking. The monasteries are not safe any longer. Especially the women's monasteries."

Caris got to her feet. "Then I am coming with the saint's people too. No one needs me at Fenwic!"

The bishop's face grew still. "There is always work for willing hands at any estate, Caris."

Edmund felt sorry for the girl Caris under the bishop's astute gaze—he had been in that place himself. After a moment, eyes downcast and speaking in a meeker voice, she said, "If you cannot keep your promise because of the Danes, then let me come with you. Please."

"So be it then," the bishop said, quite abruptly. "We stop at Fenwic only for water. Fetch everything you do not want to leave behind and be ready to go on with us." He gestured to the procession-leader with the cross, and Stitheard urged the ox pulling the cart forward again. Caris kissed the episcopal ring and dashed back along the road toward Fenwic again.

Edmund gave the bishop an inquiring look and got a little

shrug of agreement in answer, so he followed the girl. It wasn't hard to catch her up, because she couldn't keep the speed she had started with. Edmund, legs a little longer and lungs well seasoned with frequent running, could easily talk while matching her gait. "You need to pace yourself if you don't want to wear out before you finish your race, you know."

"I haven't. Got. Time!" She stopped, gasping. He could see she was on the edge of weeping, but was holding back bravely.

"Tell me who to ask for your things," said Edmund. "I'll have them ready when you get there."

Slowly she straightened and looked at him doubtfully, pale lashes clumped with tears and cheeks flushed red as rosehips. She bit her lip, then said, "The thegn's wife." She brushed her hair out of her eyes and looked away again. "She won't be sorry to see me go."

"Don't run downslope, it's too easy to trip," he suggested. "After that, run a little, walk a little. You'll still make the hall well before the coffin-bearers. You need to save some strength for after, we'll keep moving till dusk."

He turned and started off at a slow jog, but stopped when she called out, "Wait! Wait . . . Edmund, son of Tida."

"What?"

"Thank you."

"It's no trouble. I'm used to running—"

"One day you may have a reward, though!"

What an odd thing to say! "I don't need any reward."

"But you *may* have it, one day." Her chin lifted. "My mother was a princess!"

For once Edmund couldn't find anything to say. "I have to run now!" he called, and headed down the road.

FENWIC, BUCKTON, ELWIC—THEY PASSED THROUGH THE
estates in a southward line. Edmund's habit of jogging ahead
of the whole pilgrim band, sometimes with Derwin and sometimes without, ended when they left Elwic. There they turned
westward into the hills on rough, little-used tracks past isolated
shepherd's huts. The red lowering sun was glinting from the
west through the new spring leaves of the trees, hitting their
eyes every time they topped a rise now. Edmund and Derwin
had never been here on their runners' errands and had to follow
Brother Herebert, who went first, now dismounted and leading
his mare, the one horse the company possessed.

Riddle flew ahead of the line of monks, cawing a warning
to other birds in the area. The rest of the pilgrims straggled
behind, with the animals and the slow-moving coffin-cart and
other wagons bringing up the rear.

Edmund said to Derwin, "Aren't there wolves in the hills?"

Riddle swooped to Derwin's shoulder and gave his ear an
affectionate nip, and Derwin clicked his tongue in greeting to
his pet. "Riddle will warn us about those, won't you, friend?"

The bird clicked in reply and bobbed on Derwin's shoulder.
It wasn't the first time Edmund had wondered if the raven really
did understand human speech.

Edmund gripped his fishing pike tighter; it was serving as
nothing more than a walking stick now in these hills. He wished
he had the sword Derwin didn't seem to appreciate. The pike
might do against a wolf . . . but the time he visited Bebbanbyrig
with Bishop Eardwulf, he had seen the royal hall decked with
wonderful tapestries, and one of them had shown a hunter

killing a wolf with his sword. Like one warrior against another, for the beast's white teeth were sharp as knives. *No wonder people call the Danes the sea wolves!* he thought.

As they came to the top of a rocky little hill set between two higher hills, the sun turned a fiery red before them. The boys followed Herebert as he turned along a trail around the hill to the north and led them out into a grassy valley facing the small hill. But it wasn't just a hill; great slabs of sandy-gray stone lay sideways, propped on huge boulders of the same kind of stone. Above the slabs, a layer of green crowned the hill, and beneath them loomed a dark space.

"Look at that!" said Edmund. "A cave!"

"It's Saint Cuthbert's Cave," said Brother Herebert. "There have been other times when his body has been brought here to hide from raiders, for a while. The bishop and Abbot Eadred will pray there tonight. Now, see those little woods ahead to the north? You'll find a burn not far into them—take Frisk to drink, and then fetch some dry branches for the fires."

Open-mouthed, Edmund accepted the reins from his hands. But he said, "Yes, Brother!" at once and obeyed, just as he was used to obeying the bishop when sent on an errand.

The mare went willingly with Edmund, her ears pricking and nostrils widening—"Look, she hears and smells the water," Edmund said to Derwin, who walked alongside.

Riddle deserted his master's shoulder for a perch on the saddle. He sat digging his claws into the leather of the front rolled edge, chuckling to himself in satisfaction.

"Brother Herebert let me groom her once, you know," said Edmund as the mare lapped at the cool water. "If he weren't a monk, he would be a good brother."

Derwin, who was also taking a drink, wiped his mouth on his

sleeve and stood up with a rueful grin. "You get the brother you get, not the one you want."

Edmund flushed in embarrassment and handed Derwin the reins while he drank himself. But when he stood up again, he couldn't help saying, "*You* don't have to live with *my* brother!"

Derwin smiled and shrugged. They gathered a few armfuls of dry fallen branches and led Frisk back out of the woods. They found the rest of the company trickling into the open space in front of the cave. Wagons were drawn up across the entry to the clearing to the west, and halfway between there and the cave, the monks had placed rocks for a largish fire ring. Derwin scolded Riddle off his saddle-perch, and Edmund led Frisk back to her master.

Other folk had prepared smaller fire sites about the edges of the clearing, laying out sailcloth for bedding on the ground. Everywhere tired children were whining, goats bleating, and people shouting directions as they prepared to settle in for the night, men and the older boys on one side of the clearing and women and smaller children on the other. Merewyn called to them, and Edmund waved at his little sister and mother. Aelfleda and the new girl were with them. "I see your sister has taken that girl Caris under her wing, like a mother hen," he said to Derwin.

Derwin smiled. "Aelfleda does that. She'll be telling them her Saint Cuthbert tales over there tonight, I suppose. I wonder where we're headed."

"I've heard people say Norham, because Cuthbert was taken there once before for fear of raiders," said Edmund.

Then the monks began to chant, and people stopped what they were doing to cross themselves as the bearers unloaded the coffin of the saint from its cart and carried it on their shoulders up the path and into the cave. The rest of the monks crowded in after them, and the familiar sound of vespers filled the little hollow.

Hunred, of course, went into the cave with the watchers. "There goes my pretend-monk brother again," Edmund said to Derwin as they found a space to sit near some of the farm men by one of the little fires. The men were talking amongst themselves about how long the animal feed would last, and ignored the boys.

"Brother Herebert's the real thing," Edmund went on.

"Give it up, Ed." Derwin took some dried apples out of his bag and handed one to Edmund.

Edmund frowned and rummaged in his own pack for a dried fish, which he gave to Derwin. Chewing his apple, Edmund let his thoughts continue to trickle out. "It wouldn't be so bad being a monk if you had Brother Herebert's job."

Derwin, who was feeding bits of his fish to Riddle, looked at him in surprise. "Were you thinking of being a monk?"

"Me? No! I'm a fisherman." *Like my father,* Edmund almost said, and then didn't.

chapter six

EDMUND WOKE WHEN THE DAWN TURNED THE MIST pale and began to melt it. The caged rooster on one of the wagons crowed from the western end of the clearing, and to the east a stir of muffled activity at the cave drew Edmund's attention. The men and boys nearby grunted and moaned, not ready to rise. Edmund got to his feet quietly and made his way toward the monks. Their camp by the cave emerged from the mist, and Edmund saw that many of them were still curled up asleep too. And then none other than Hunred emerged from the black mouth of the cave.

Edmund's brother looked directly at him but said not a word, only turned aside to shake one of the monks awake, speaking low in his ear. The monk sat up—it was Herebert. To Edmund's great irritation, Hunred then spoke to Herebert in the sign language used at the monastery during the times that required silence. Edmund had never mastered more than the signs for passing bread or salt at meals.

Hunred went back to the cave without a backward glance,

but as he rose and stretched, Brother Herebert spotted Edmund and smiled, motioning him to join him on the path that led westward away from the cave. When they had left the monks behind, they quickened their pace.

"Can I help you saddle Frisk?" Edmund begged as they passed through the slowly stirring layfolk, men on their left and women on their right.

"All right then. Thank you."

The chickens were chattering, and goats began bleating to be milked as Edmund and Herebert continued on to where the mare was tethered to a stake in the ground beyond the wagons.

"So where are we going now?" Edmund finally dared ask when Herebert had shown him how to check the girth straps.

The monk hiked up his habit to clamber into the saddle. "Across this valley to those hills. An estate called Horton, a little south and west of here. The hall overlooks the River Till to the south and the old Roman road to the east. Depending on what news we get there, we hope soon to begin making for Mailros—by what roads we must wait and see."

"Mailros!" It was a famous monastery, the one Saint Cuthbert himself had ridden up to on his horse as a youth, and seeing him Saint Boisil had said, "Behold the servant of the Lord!" "But isn't Mailros days and days away, far up the River Tweed?"

Herebert gently tugged the reins to turn the mare's head westward. "Maybe weeks, with a company the size of this one."

"Can I come part way with you now? I can keep up!"

Herebert laughed. "Why not? Only an hour, mind—then you must run back."

He touched the horse's sides lightly with his heels and she went off at a walk, Edmund easily jogging alongside.

And then the trees closed in. The sun rose behind them, and the sky showed pale blue between the skeletal branches above, bejeweled with bright spring buds. Edmund had to follow along behind Frisk on the narrowed path. It looked like there would barely be room for the wagons on it. It did not go on for long, but Brother Herebert reined in Frisk as they reached an opening, then dismounted, a finger on his lips to Edmund. He handed Edmund the reins and then inched forward to peer out, checking all directions before he nodded to Edmund.

They came out onto a road edged with brambles on this side and coppiced hazel on the other. Edmund had seen coppicing on the lands nearer Lindesfarne, and knew this was a sign they could not be too far from a settlement. The young hazels had been cut down to allow many new shoots called withies to sprout up from the stumps. The estate's woodmen would come out here to cut the withies for building and repairing sheds and huts on the estate. But the dirt surface of the road was dry and half grown over with chickweed and plantain down the center of the tracks, which were not deep. So this road was not used often. Herebert had taught Edmund to note such signs when he first showed him the messenger ways at home.

Rooks called from the treetops, and small animals rustled amongst last year's crumbling leaves. In the quiet, Edmund could hear the trickle of a burn westward just beyond the coppiced trees.

Brother Herebert remounted. "Horton is this way," he said, turning Frisk's head to face south along the road, which went on for a furlong or more before curving away to the west out of sight. "Now, Edmund, you go back and tell the bishop that I should be back by noon to say if they can receive us."

Edmund watched horse and rider jog away southward. *Clop-*

clop. Jingle. To ride a horse—it was almost like being a thegn and warrior!

Clop-clop. Jingle. Herebert suddenly drew his mount up in the center of the road. More faintly: *clop-clop, jingle clop jingle clop-clop . . .* hoofbeats approached from up around the bend. Hoofbeats and voices, raised in raucous laughter and a spirited exchange of some kind.

Brother Herebert glanced over his shoulder and saw Edmund still standing there. Frowning, he waved him back into the trees.

Edmund stood openmouthed, rooted to the spot as Herebert turned again, ready to face the approaching strangers. The voices were louder now. Edmund could hear the words, but could not make them out.

Suddenly Herebert tugged on the reins sharply. Frisk gave a little whinny of protest as she turned in response, and then her rider dug his heels into her sides in a way Edmund had never seen him do before, clicked his tongue and cried "Gee-yah!" Like an arrow from a bow, the mare shot straight and fast along the road to the north, away from the approaching riders. A shout went up from the strangers. As Herebert passed, he turned his head toward Edmund long enough to mouth, "Hide!"

Edmund's heart pounded. The path that had seemed so narrow before now felt open and exposed, and he plunged into the woods to the north of it, scrambling to put at least a few rods' distance between him and the path before he fell to the ground behind the screen of old blackened brambles that edged the road. A moment later three mounted warriors came thundering past in a flash of color and metal, just visible through the curtain of brambles.

"Halt!" one of them boomed, but followed that recognizable

word with a speech that sounded almost like real words and yet made no sense to Edmund. *Because it's Danske*, he thought. *They are Danes . . . run, Frisk!*

Quickly the galloping hooves moved out of Edmund's hearing along the road. Dry-mouthed, he began to make his way northward through the woods. Terror of being seen kept him working his way along behind the bramble screen, pausing to listen now and then.

When he was on the point of despairing and turning back, he heard horses returning, more slowly this time. The Danish voices were cheery and relaxed now, chuckling instead of guffawing. Edmund searched frantically for a viewpoint in the brambles and found one he could use from a kneeling position. The men and horses came near, and he peered out at the horses' girth-level as they passed: one, two, three sets of wool-and-leather-clad legs on horseback . . . and one riderless horse. A chestnut horse with a black tail . . .

Edmund's throat closed up. He waited till they had passed south and then gritted his teeth to crawl through the bramble opening, ignoring the scratches on his fingers and cursing under his breath at the way his woolen clothing caught. Just before the riders went out of sight around the bend towards Horton again, he confirmed his fear: they had taken Frisk, but Herebert was not with them.

He turned north and ran. The road curved slowly to the left as he pounded along one track, his sure feet avoiding any turning of the ankles on the tussocks of grass and weed. Then the road straightened. A few rods ahead, a dark heap lay in the center of the road.

Edmund stopped dead, his pulse throbbing in his throat and breath coming short as it never did when he ran errands for the bishop. *Finish the race! Finish the race!* The same three words ran through his head, over and over. His feet did not want to obey the command. Finally he moved them, one at a time, breaking the spell. *Now run,* he told himself, and he did.

He came to a stop at Herebert's feet, chest aching. The monk lay face down. By his head and shoulders a stain, still bright red, spread across the clumps of weed and dirt track.

"Brother Herebert?" Edmund's voice came out in a hoarse whisper.

A messenger had to be sure he had real information, all he could get, to take back. A messenger couldn't shrink from turning over a man who was . . .

Dead. Edmund knew it before he even shook the monk's shoulder. So much blood . . . it *might* only be a bloody nose, where the Danes had thrown him to the ground to take his horse. But Herebert was too still.

My friend. My brother. Brother Herebert. With a sob Edmund fell down at Herebert's side, took hold of his shoulder and rolled him over. Then he made himself look, even while his own blood seemed to turn to ice in his veins.

It was not just a smashed nose. It was a cut, clean and deep, through the throat. A killing slice from a warrior's dagger, efficient as a butcher's. They wanted the horse, they took the horse, and killed the monk. *I wish it had been Hunred instead!* The dreadful thought tore at Edmund's heart with claws of grief, anger, and guilt. A wordless wail rose up in him and rang out to the sky above the empty road.

Edmund did not stir from the spot for he knew not how long. At some point he became aware of a silence in the woods, and then of the gradual return of the chirruping and calling of birds, the scolding of squirrels.

"Kah-kah-kah!" The rooks in the trees bobbed and fanned their tails. Edmund flung them an angry look and yelled, "Stop it!" but they paid no attention.

Then there was a loud call of "Cronk!" from above. A larger black bird dove into the trees, flapping and scolding. The rooks took flight in alarm. The raven gave one more "Cronk!" and took off again. It circled above, then flew down to perch on Edmund's shoulder.

"Riddle!" It came out as a sob. Gratefully Edmund stroked the bird's throat with his forefinger. Riddle imitated the higher-pitched 'kah-kah-kah!' of the rooks and gave what was almost a little growl of disapproval in his throat.

The sun beat down. Edmund was still gulping back tears, but he thought, *I have to run and warn them. I have a race to finish.*

Making the sign of the cross, he reached out and closed Brother Herebert's eyes. Then he stood up. "Let's go, Riddle."

chapter seven

N0 *THINKING*. R*IDDLE HAD FLOWN OFF THE MOMENT* Edmund got up. The raven had disappeared over the treetops eastward, and now Edmund fastened his eyes on the road ahead. *No thinking, finish the race.* He found the trail and dove in. He leapt over tree roots and ducked under low-hanging branches, on through the sun-dappled tunnel.

He heard the raven call overhead. And then he saw Derwin coming toward him, framed by the arch of trees at the end of the trail.

"Ed! Where have you been?"

Edmund ran on till they met, then paused, heaving breaths, deep and steady with the rhythm of his run. He could not speak, but gave his puzzled friend a helpless look and ran on.

He burst into the open. Past men checking animals' hooves and tightening lines on laden wagons, past the remains of the night's camp with the dying fires. Past his little sister Merewyn, who shouted, "Eddie! Mother is so angry with you!"

He shoved his way into the cave amongst habited bodies

packed close, the drone of a psalm filling the space with a sea of sound Edmund could feel to the core of his being. He tumbled through the packed assembly and fell against the coffin of Saint Cuthbert itself. Bishop Eardwulf stood there in his stole, a look of shock on his face.

Edmund's tongue finally loosed itself. "Brother Herebert—the Danes—they've killed him!"

The chanting died. The silence almost hurt Edmund's ears. His knees felt weak, and he must have looked as if he might fall down, for Bishop Eardwulf gently took him by the elbow to ease him away from the holy coffin, supporting him instead with his own arm. "Bring water," the bishop said, and a moment later one of the monks put a waterskin to Edmund's lips.

Edmund drank, wiped his mouth, and gave his report: "Three mounted warriors from the south—from Horton. Herebert told me to hide. I heard them shouting—not in our language. They chased him north. Then they came back with Frisk—but no Herebert. I waited till it was safe, then I found him." Just for a moment he faltered, then went on: "In the road. With his throat cut."

Gasps and *misereres*. Signs of the cross. The bishop looked grim.

Sometimes, back home on Lindesfarne, Edmund would walk up to the rocky hill called Beblow Crag that raised itself up above the flat plain of the rest of the island, where you could look south along the curving bay of Lindesfarne harbor. You would see, far away and tiny, familiar people doing familiar things—children beachcombing, women chatting with their neighbors. But you didn't hear anything except the wind buffeting your ears, and the surf washing against the base of the crag.

It was like that now for Edmund, but instead of up on the

crag in the fresh sea air, he was somewhere far inside himself. The people who spoke to him seemed far away and small, and he heard only a rushing in his ears. Someone took him by the arm and led him out of the cave. Someone embraced him with a sob, and after a bit he realized it was his mother. He wasn't sure if she had scolded him yet.

When she stepped back, he saw that Derwin was there too, and Merewyn and Aelfleda and the girl called Caris. And standing behind the others was Hunred. That wasn't right—*he* ought to be with the coffin-bearers. "Go away," Edmund said to him. Hardly a flicker of response crossed Hunred's face, and he did not move, though the others looked at him.

"Edmund," said the girl Caris, "I have some hazelnut cake, here, eat it."

But his mother shouldered her aside and shook him. "Edmund! You will not speak to your elder brother like that!"

"He needs to eat, after running all that way!" said Caris.

"Hssht, come away!" said Aelfleda, and pulled the impudent stranger girl off. "Derwin, you too!"

The scolding continued, with Merewyn standing by teary-eyed, and Hunred impassive as usual. The *running off without telling anyone*, the *never thinking for one moment* about the *frantic worry of his mother!*

But scolding couldn't go on forever, when the one being scolded stood there without moving a muscle. Finally his mother let him go and stood glaring at him with her hands on her hips.

Edmund slowly drew himself up, meeting her gaze. "I am not a child any more," he said, in a cold and measured voice, and her eyes widened in surprise. "I am a messenger of the bishop, and I am the man of this family." He turned on Hunred. "You don't belong here, go back to your *holy* work!"

Hunred looked at him for a moment more, then made a little bow of the head to their mother, turned, and went without another word.

"Hunred!" she called after him, but he kept going. Other people nearby stared a moment at the family drama, then turned away in embarrassment.

Edmund stalked off, heading for the little burn where he and Derwin had watered Frisk . . . was that only yesterday? He felt suddenly dizzy. Quickly he stooped down to cup the water in his hands, first to drink and then to splash over his face. His hands were trembling. All through his run he had tried not to think; now he knew he *should* think, but didn't want to. The feelings were so big and so many, like sheep trying to crowd through a gate together, that he couldn't catch hold of any of them.

Soon Derwin joined him and gave him a piece of dried fish. "Your mother sent this."

Edmund took the fish, grunting noncommittally.

"And this you'll maybe want to save in your travel-bag for time of need." Derwin handed Edmund a little packet of something wrapped in waxed linen. "Hazelnut-cake made with honey, it'll keep a long time. From Caris. I think she likes you."

Edmund looked at Derwin's sly smile and rolled his eyes. "No, she doesn't. It's her gracious *reward* for me helping her before. She says her mother is a king's daughter!"

Derwin shrugged. "Ed, some monks have gone to bring Herebert back. They'll soon sing memorial and bury him by the cave."

And Hunred would be there, hands folded in his sleeves and eyes raised to the pale silent heaven above this dreadful world, where fathers didn't come home from the sea and mild, kind monks ended on a dusty road with cut throats. Hunred would be at the service, playing monk, or his idea of a monk.

"I'm not coming," Edmund said, almost choking.

After the merest pause, Derwin said, "All right," and put an arm around Edmund while tears leaked out from the shuddering dam of his tight-clenched eyelids.

After a long while, Riddle circled above them, cawing, then alighted on Edmund's head and promptly relieved himself with a loud squawk. Edmund let out a wordless curse, then joined Derwin in helpless laughter.

HAIR WASHED, COMBED, AND NEATLY REBRAIDED, EDMUND answered a summons from the bishop when the memorial chant ended. A monk brought him to the cave, where Bishop Eardwulf was seated on a bundle of belongings in front of the saint's coffin, Abbot Eadred and Stitheard flanking him.

"How goes it with you now, Edmund?" said the bishop.

"I have had food and water, my lord bishop. I can run anywhere you want to send me."

The bishop's brows rose. "I would not send a man out on another errand after enduring what you endured today, Edmund."

Edmund swallowed and nodded. He felt like his heart was being torn in two—one way with grief for Brother Herebert, another with pride to be called a man by the bishop.

"So these three Danes were headed north when they found Herebert," said the bishop. "They likely only turned back long enough to stable the horse they killed him for."

"My guess is, they have taken Horton," said Stitheard.

Suddenly Abbot Eadred spoke up. "My brothers, I believe we must leave the roads entirely."

"Leave the roads!" the reeve said.

But the bishop took a deep breath and nodded. "Yes. As we thought—these Danes are here not to rob and leave, but to take our lands for themselves. They have taken horses from the people about the Tyne, and now they will travel the length and breadth of the land, over the straight roads made long ago by Rome."

"Yet they are not Rome," said Eadred. "This Halfdan who styles himself their war-leader does not hold all their allegiance. Their force is made up of small bands from many lands, each out for their own profit. They have no great plan to work and conquer as one. We could meet any number of them at any time. So we should stay off the easy roads—but to get to the hills, we must cross the Devil's Causeway near Horton whether we will or no."

"Devil's Causeway!" Edmund couldn't help bursting out.

"Only a name, Edmund, given to it by ignorant folk who do not know how the great Empire was able to build a straight road that runs from the Wall of Hadrian by the Tyne in the south all the way to the Tweed in the north. There will be a moon tonight. Beneath it, if God and Saint Cuthbert are with us, we will cross the Devil's Causeway and pass Horton without the Danes' knowing, then north onto Doddington moor, and from there plan our road westward."

Eadred nodded and Stitheard sighed in resignation, but once again Edmund could not help speaking: "But the holy cart! The ox! And the baggage wagons—will these hill-paths take them?"

The men all looked at Edmund, and he wished he had held his tongue.

"Edmund," said Bishop Aerdwulf, "The body of the saint is more holy than the cart it lies upon. We ourselves, all of us from Lindesfarne, are the haliwerfolc, the holy saint's holy people. The ox and cart will take our saint a long way yet, I think. But if we must bear him upon our own very shoulders," he said, and on Edmund's shoulder he laid a hand, "then bear him we shall."

chapter eight

THE PROCESSION WENT SILENTLY BY THE RISING half-moon, and under Bishop Eardwulf's stern order against any talking, making do without lanterns along the wooded path toward the Horton road. The animals didn't like it, and bleated or lowed or dug in their heels when their masters tried to urge them forward beneath the black skeletal branches.

Edmund didn't like it either. He plodded along, fish pike in hand and Merewyn at his side, for he had promised his mother he would look after her. It was a relief when they emerged onto the open road, away from the grasping branches and tree-roots underfoot. Southwestward they went, straggling behind the quick-stepping bishop and two of his monks, while the coffin-attendants and other wagons again brought up the rear. The golden processional cross was now put somewhere safely away with the candlesticks and other church treasures, such as the jewel-covered Gospel book.

Not far around the curve where the three Danes had first

appeared that morning, they splashed through a small chuck-ling burn. The trees flanking the road gave way to fields, and Edmund heard the rushing of a larger river, the Till, Herebert had called it, downslope to the left. Rising from the bank came a road, straight and covered with wide flat stones. They were in ill repair and had weeds growing between them, but Edmund shuddered as they clattered across the surface of what could only be the Roman road called the Devil's Causeway.

As they crossed, suddenly the sound of song and laughter made him look up to the right. The others heard it too, and the procession slowed. Perched on the long slope above them was a hall which must be Horton. Light leaked out between the tim-bers of its doors, and smoke billowed, white in the moonlight, from the smokehole in the high-peaked thatched roof.

"Hsst!" Ahead, Bishop Eardwulf motioned them on across the Roman road, and as quickly as they could the company fol-lowed the path westward alongside the north riverbank, past a dank little wood where mist was beginning to curl. Then around behind the wood to the right and along a sheep track that skirted the lower slope of the wide hill, then began to climb. As the moon mounted ever higher in the sky behind them, the company too mounted steadily along the track laid out in front of them over an open moor.

Above the world and away from the sound of the hall that was likely now held by enemies, the company breathed relief, and when quiet talk welled up the bishop no longer silenced them, till a barking and snarling arose ahead.

"Who goes?" called a rough voice. "Ware, my dogs will have you!"

Edmund pushed forward, his grip tightening on the pike. But it was only a shepherd, who called his dogs to heel at once when he learned who they were. The sheep continued to bleat worriedly while they talked with him.

"A band of Danes took Horton hall two days ago," he told them. "Killed the lord and his few men, now they're living off the hall folk and planning what to do next. They haven't troubled me, but I'm afraid they'll attack Doddington to the north next."

"We'll be off at sunrise," said the bishop. "And pass Doddington without stopping."

The moon was westering, and with the shepherd's guidance the company straggled up atop the windy moor and settled as best they could for a few hours' rest. The monks gathered round the holy coffin, but no one troubled to separate the camps of men and women as they had at the cave, the people gathering instead in small family groups. The wind dropped, but the air took on a damp chill, and soon mist was gathering around them. With no supper and no fires, it was worse than the night before.

The crowd fell silent, and Edmund drifted to sleep with the chanting of nocturnes in his ears.

Something woke him. The fog hadn't thinned much, but it had lightened just a little—false dawn, or real? He thought he heard movement off to the right . . . then he saw the winking of a golden light. He stood up, snatching up his spear, and stepped over his sleeping sister to follow it.

He prowled closer to the cloaked figure. No taller than himself—Edmund's breath caught as he drew close enough, on the figure's left flank, to see the tin lantern. He recognized the tin X bracing the panes of thinly sliced horn that let out the light while protecting the flame. "That's mine!" he cried.

The lantern-holder gasped and turned in startlement. Caris!

"My father bought that lantern from a traveling tinker when

I was only small!" Edmund raged. "It cost us *three farthings* that took us *ages* to save!"

"I'm only borrowing it," said the girl, frowning.

"You never *asked*! And how did you light it?"

"I used Derwin's tinder box. He won't mind. *He* likes me."

Edmund stood furious and openmouthed. Caris glared back at him, not giving an inch. Then she appeared to change course.

"Do you want to see something no one else noticed on the way up?"

Edmund gave her a wary look. There was something worth seeing, he was sure, or Caris would not have troubled to "borrow" the lantern and tinderbox, work at lighting the candle, and creep out here away from the comforting nearness of the company.

"Didn't you think about wolves?" he snapped.

She flinched momentarily, but then said, "They won't come around here, that shepherd and his dogs will have them cowed."

"You don't know any such thing!"

"Do you want to come see or not?"

"Not. And I'll have my lantern back."

Caris pursed her lips and thrust the lantern at him, turned on her heel and marched off into the mist. Only a dozen steps away, the fog swallowed her completely.

Edmund ground his teeth. *She'll get lost in no time!* He sprinted after her, heedless of the rough ground beneath his feet.

"*You* carry the light," he growled. "I'll keep watch for wolves," he added, patting the haft of his fishing pike. He pretended not to see the smug smile as she took the lantern and led the way.

The lantern did not help a great deal. Edmund's patience was wearing thin when Caris started to look worried.

"It's stupid, stumbling around in this fog. We can come back and look in the morning," he said, trying to sound reasonable like Derwin.

Caris whispered, "Look," and held up the lantern.

A dark shape loomed ahead in the murk, taller than a tall man and much wider, square like a door.

For a moment they both stood rooted to the ground.

"What is it?" Edmund asked finally, his voice hoarse.

"My mother's people called them Long Men. Standing stones, set up long, long ago."

"Like the road we just crossed?"

"The Devil's Causeway, you mean?" said Caris, cool and superior.

Annoyance swept away Edmund's nerves. "The bishop says ignorant people call it that. The Romans built it, not the devil."

"Maybe he didn't build it. Maybe he just travels on it," she said, her voice low, and in spite of himself Edmund felt the hair rise on the back of his neck.

"We'd better worry about the Danes traveling on it instead," he spat. "So what are we here for?"

"I'll show you," she said, tossing her head.

Edmund followed. "There are more!" He turned around in the billowing mist, while Caris raised the lantern. "A circle!"

"Yes. A circle. My mother's people used to know secret lore. They could tell things by looking at the sun and moon and stars from these circles."

There was no end to how irritating the girl could be. "Your mother's people! What people?"

"The Cymraeg," she said, chin in the air, looking at the stones instead of at Edmund. "The Romans killed the sages who knew about the circles. And then the Angles and Saxons killed most of the rest of us!"

Edmund bristled. "You're an Angle yourself!" Now he knew who she was talking about—the people she called Cymraeg were the Wealas—the slave people. Well, she *had* been a slave, he was sure, before the bishop took her on—but the Wealas lived far beyond the hills to the west, those that hadn't been made captive by the Angles who were Edmund's ancestors. Any Wealas he had ever seen, serving as freemen now on Lindesfarne lands, were short folk with square faces and dark hair, not tall and fair like most Angles. Like himself, and like Caris with her red-gold hair.

Caris gave him a disdainful look and then changed the subject. "I thought we might see an omen looking at the sunrise between the stones."

Edmund frowned at the mention of omens. The bishop hadn't rebuked people for *calling* it an omen when Riddle flew toward the mainland. But the monks always discouraged people from purposefully *looking* for omens. "We'd better go back—" Edmund stared suddenly about. The stones . . . some were odd-shaped, but several were fairly rectangular, like the first one they had seen. Which way led back to the company?

Caris pulled her cloak closer, her face suddenly uncertain.

"That way," said Caris, pointing across the circle at one of the square-topped stones.

"You're sure?"

For answer she stalked away, and Edmund again followed, grumbling.

The downhill slope away from the stone circle went on longer than Edmund remembered the upward climb taking. The mist thickened again. He was suddenly angry with himself—

following Caris and made prickly by her behavior, he had utterly forgotten his messenger habits!

Without warning they landed in water up to their calves. Edmund cursed loudly. "This isn't the way!"

A little gasp escaped Caris. She held up the lantern, but they couldn't see much. It was a bog, of course—they should have known from the smell. They turned around, but after a short climb found themselves going down again, and the mire appeared at their feet once more. This time Caris looked really frightened, and Edmund stopped being annoyed with her.

"It's all right," he said firmly. "We'll go upward again as far as we can, then just stop and listen." Silently he prayed, *Holy Father Cuthbert, guide us to your coffin!*

Already, as they plodded back upslope, the fog looked like a daytime fog and not a nighttime fog any more, but it was thick and opaque as milk still. Would it muffle sound as well as sight? Would they be able to hear the monks chanting prime?

Edmund didn't want to call for help. His mother would again scold him about going off without telling anyone, and he dared not think what the bishop would say.

"We're back!" cried Caris. Back at the stone circle, she meant. And at the base of one of the stones opposite, Edmund saw a shadow move. As Caris lifted the lantern, the light caught and reflected from two glowing eyes. With a gasp she grabbed hold of Edmund's sleeve. He tightened his grip on his spear. And then the candle in the lantern guttered.

"*Kyrie eleison!*" Edmund breathed.

He shook off Caris's hand and planted himself in front of her, brandishing the pike. His throat felt like it was closing up on him, and his hands shook on the haft of the pike. The shadow advanced, a gray muzzle emerging from the mist as it paced toward them. Its jaws opened in a tongue-lolling smile, just like any of the dogs at Lindesfarne hall, as it paused to regard them critically. But it wasn't a dog.

"Wait till it jumps at me," Edmund told Caris, without taking his eyes off the wolf. "Then run for your life—run anywhere, and shout for help!"

The wolf's yellow eyes narrowed, its tongue drew back, and a low growl issued from between its bared teeth. Edmund breathed, "Cuthbert, help!" and gripped his pike tighter.

The wolf's ears pricked, and it paused for a moment, listening. Then, abruptly, it turned and ran off the way it had come.

Edmund's heart was beating so loudly that a few moments passed before he heard, somewhere in the mist behind him, what the wolf had heard: a solo voice singing clear and deep a hymn he knew well from the short time he'd spent at the monastic school.

"*Iam lucis ordo sidere, Deum precemur supplices. . . .*"

The singing grew rapidly louder, and Edmund called out, "Waes hal, Brother!"

"Good morning to you," came the reply.

The monk who stepped out of the fog was Abbot Eadred of Luel. Caris leapt forward to kiss his hand.

"Holy father abbot, we were lost!" she said.

Eadred nodded kindly at them both. "Come back with me now." And he set off, resuming the hymn at the next line, "*Ut in diurnis actibus, Nos servet a nocentibus.*"

By the end of a meager breakfast of more dried fish, the glimmering sun had melted most of the mist, and a rising wind came to tear off the last shreds of it. Edmund took Derwin aside while the company assembled for the day's march. With Riddle circling above them, they walked a distance west of the company and stopped in a dry spot, where hard bare stone poked up through the peaty soil of the moor beneath their feet. Edmund told Derwin about Caris and the stones and the wolf and the abbot.

"Saint Cuthbert saved you," said Derwin. "You prayed for his help, and he sent Abbot Eadred to find you!"

For once Edmund didn't want to keep talking. The awe of Saint Cuthbert and God and the miraculously timely arrival of Abbot Eadred made his stomach flutter. He gazed up to the horizon, uncloaked by the vanishing morning fog, and sudden dismay crept in to pierce the awe and gratitude. "Look at the height of those hills!"

Derwin looked too. "I think . . . I think there's still snow on the tops."

After a moment, Edmund set his hands on his hips and drew himself up. Abbot Eadred had given him a second chance. He was going to serve the bishop as messenger again, and he was not going to be afraid of anything that would greet them in the strange new country where they were headed. "We'll be all right. The bishop and abbot will lead us. We'll be all right."

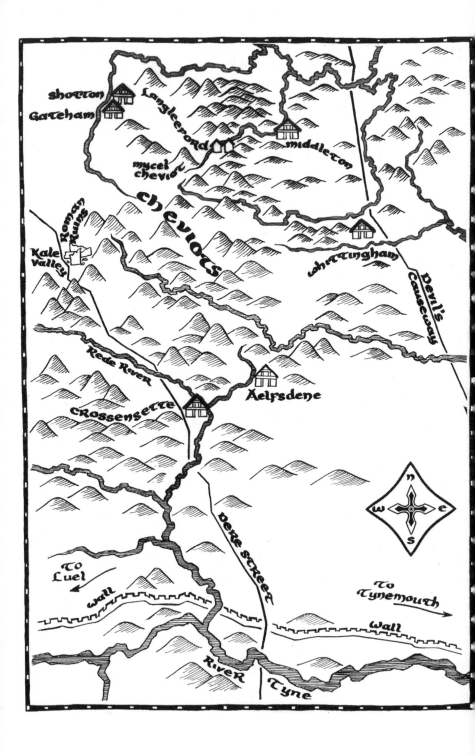

shotton
Gateham
Langleeford
mycel cheviot
middleton
cheviots
Roman Ruins
Kale valley
whittingham
Devil's Causeway
Rede River
crossensette
Aelfsdene
Dere Street
to Luel
wall
to Tynemouth
wall
River Tyne

Part II

The Cheviot Hills

A.D. 878

chapter nine

"COME ON, DERWIN!" EAGERLY EDMUND TOPPED THE final rise of the Mycel Cheviot, the highest point in the hills. The boggy ground of the wide summit pulled at his feet, but that scarcely slowed him. Despite the pack on his back and the long-shafted fishing spear in his hand, he nearly felt he could fly. The day they had left Doddington Moor, Edmund had learned from Abbot Eadred to imagine himself as a skylark hovering high above the ground, looking out at all the world spread below him. On this windy height, the imagination was almost reality. Riddle flew ahead of them, as if he knew the way; Edmund was going by the memory of careful observation coupled with instruction from the abbot, who knew these hills well.

It was some three years now since they had left the lands near Lindesfarne, and nearly the whole time the company had been hunted, hungry, tired, and sometimes sick. Their discouraging pilgrimage had taken them back and forth among the hills and valleys, forests and moors of the north. Edmund did not mind the hardship, though. He was a messenger for the bishop. After the Danes killed Herebert, the bishop had started sending Edmund and Derwin along with other monks and laymen to scout between the company's resting places. But now he and Derwin were older and had learned much of the country, and this was their first scouting foray on their own. And though dangerous weather and the threat of wandering groups of Danes were always in the offing, still Edmund loved it, every minute.

He turned again to call, "Derwin!" His friend never set the pace, but mostly he kept up with Edmund. This time, though, he had been lagging, and now Edmund saw him bent over, hands on his thighs. "What, are you caught in the bog there?"

Derwin straightened, shaking his head, lips pressed tight and dark brows drawn together in his pale face. Alarmed, Edmund splashed back to him.

"It's just the growing pains in my knees, my father says," said Derwin with a sigh. "Have you not had them too?"

"Not so badly." Opposite Derwin, Edmund realized he now had to look up to his friend, who seemed to be taking after his tall father. "My legs hurt some last winter, when we were staying at Mailros with not much running to do. Come on, let's get to the other side—we can rest while we look out over the land."

Groaning, Derwin joined him. At the eastern edge of the height, Derwin slung off his pack and began to root in it. "It's a wonder we've grown at all," said Derwin. "My stomach hasn't felt full since the Christ Mass."

Edmund stared at the misty blue horizon in disappointment. Unseen beyond a sheep-dotted slope in the middle distance, beyond plains and moors and woods, somewhere to the northeast was Lindesfarne.

"Here." Derwin handed him a piece of hard hazelnut cake.

"Caris made it." Riddle swooped down, loudly demanding a share, to perch on Derwin's shoulder while Derwin broke him a piece. Then he took off his father's sword, which he wore slung over his back too, and sat down on his pack.

Setting down his fishing spear, Edmund eyed the jet-and-silver pommel of the sword as he could never help doing, ashamed as always of his envy. He undid his own pack and sat down on it beside Derwin, nibbling the gritty honey-sweetened cake.

"You know, she's worriting herself about going back to Aelfsdene," said Derwin. He looked vaguely out on the hills and plains spread before them.

Edmund pointed past him to the right, over the next hill. "Aelfsdene is south. But the company may not end up going there."

The bishop had sent them out from the company's camp at Gateham to gather news at Langleeford, a short way to the east now. There were rumors of Danes in the area, and the company, while hoping to presume on the hospitality of the people of Gateham through the remainder of the autumn, would have to move on after the Christ Mass. Aelfsdene, where the company hoped to find welcome and perhaps settle, was days farther south.

"Aelfsdene was where Caris was a slave?" Edmund asked. "Did they treat her badly?"

"It's complicated, I think. But not for me to say. Anyway . . ." Derwin took a deep breath, and without looking at Edmund, said, "I've made up my mind to marry her."

"Marry her!" The shock was like a storm wave washing over a boat. "You can't marry Caris! You—well—you're the reeve's son, practically a thegn! And she, she was a slave—"

Derwin looked at him. "Edmund, haven't you noticed—we're

all of us poor and homeless and landless. I already spoke to my father. He's asking the bishop."

It was a good thing Edmund was sitting down; it seemed like the world was suddenly spinning. "Yes, we're poor—we don't even have enough food and clothing in the company. Everywhere we go, no one takes us in for long. People can't be getting married when things are like this!"

"Ed," Derwin said patiently, "we had two weddings last summer at Gedwearde, remember? And then there were those three families that left us after Mailros . . . you're right, there's no food or home for a company this size. I want to take Caris and go to her mother's people in the Wealas country."

"That's mad!" Edmund stood up, unable to stay put any longer. "How will you get there?"

Derwin glared up at him. "On our feet, the same way we get everywhere else."

"Don't tell me you believe that nonsense she says about being a princess!"

For a moment their flaming gazes met, and the wind whistled around them. Derwin looked away first, swallowing. "Ed, she *is* Wealisc. Or at least her mother was. She has to have kinfolk *somewhere* there."

"And how will you find them?"

"Edmund!" Derwin jumped to his feet, setting Riddle off into a scold. "I'm going to do it! Wouldn't a friend wish me well?"

Edmund took a ragged breath. "No. A friend wouldn't let you do anything so stupid!"

Derwin picked up his pack. "You can't stop me."

Edmund too picked up his pack and pike, and they walked on in cold silence for a time, Riddle coming and going at whim. It was only when they reached the top of the next hill that Derwin said, "I was going to ask you to come with us."

Edmund kept walking, staring at the sheep track that led them down into the wooded valley below. "I can't leave Saint Cuthbert," he said at last.

There was a moment's silence as Edmund walked on and Derwin paused. Then Derwin called from behind, "Since when are you so holy-minded? You never go to the services, and just last night by the fire you were complaining about Hunred and his pious looks, the way you always have!"

Edmund turned, feeling his cheeks go hot. "I know," he admitted. "But I . . . I have to finish the race, Derwin. All the way to the end, however long it takes. That day at the stone circle with the wolf, when Abbot Eadred came and found me—I got a second chance that day. And Caris too. Maybe she's got kin elsewhere, but I don't. I've got Merewyn and my mother with the company."

A cry of *Waes hal!* echoed out across the valley, and they both looked down the slope to see a young shepherd boy mounting towards them, quick and nimble as a goat, wearing a ragged, grubby tunic that once must have been the fine black-and-white check favored by the hill folk. Two shaggy black-and-white dogs tagged at his heels, tongues lolling eagerly.

"Did you hear the news? Halfdan the chief of the Danes is dead!"

THERE WAS NO HALL AT LANGLEEFORD, JUST A COLLECTION of stone shepherd's *botls*; their flocks belonged to the lord of Middleton, downstream. Edmund and Derwin sat with a half-dozen of the rough, dirty shepherd men and boys around the open hearth in one botl, hearing a tale of the Dane chieftain's downfall that seemed to grow wilder with each round of the thick beer.

"God gave that heathen what for, He did!" said one of the men. "Halfdan went mad, and only three ships of men would follow him to Ireland."

"And he stank," one of the boys added with relish. "His flesh rotted on him while he was still alive!"

The grisly tale only added to the joy of feasting on a sheep that had, apparently, fallen in the burn and broken its neck. Edmund licked his fingers, savoring the rich, satisfying taste and the fullest belly he had known for a long time. Until the chief shepherd noted with a wink that he wasn't going to let his *jarl* know about it.

Edmund's heart sank. *Jarl* was what the Danes called their lords of thegn rank. "So the Danes rule you here now?"

"Oh, so they do, since Lammas—a month and a fortnight gone now. When Halfdan dared call himself king at Eoforwic two years ago, he parceled out land all over Northumbria to his followers."

"Yes, but wasn't that mostly around Eoforwic?" Eoforwic was far south, below the Tyne and Hadrian's wall.

"Ah, but the great heathen host is no more," said the man, "split into many little war-bands now. Here and there along the coast and plain, a daring jarl and his few warriors find they can take a little place like our Middleton—this bold beggar even married the widowed lady to make it easier to hold it!"

"Do you know if they hold Aelfsdene?" asked Derwin.

But the rustic men had only a foggy understanding of any place beyond Middleton.

Aelfsdene's young lord had been friendly toward Lindesfarne before the Danes arrived. The company might get there by heading down the Devil's Causeway. But should they risk meeting Danes in places along the causeway in the plain? Or take the high way instead, the steep and wearying way southward along the spine of the Cheviot hills, much of it far from any settlements where they might find food and shelter?

Well, things might change over the winter, thought Edmund. And then it would be for Bishop Eardwulf to decide.

AT MIDDAY NEXT DAY, THEY SLOGGED THROUGH THE MUCKY ground on the way back to the company at Gateham. When the autumn-chilled drizzle turned to hard rain, Riddle traveled hunched on Derwin's shoulder. Again and again Edmund turned to find his friend falling behind, moving with obvious discomfort. The rainclouds darkened with a promise to bring the night early.

Suddenly the raven launched from his perch with a *quork!* and flapped up to sit on a broken stone wall that lay before them in the mist. Two entirely unfamiliar large piles of stone, widely separated, flanked the wall. Edmund cursed himself for an idiot, and Derwin's eyes went wide with panic.

"How long ago did we turn wrong?" Edmund asked.

Derwin shook his head hopelessly. He looked the picture of misery, rain beading on his shapeless wool cap and streaming from the rolled brim down his face.

Edmund turned about, straining for a familiar landmark. The hills had turned to gray-green shadows behind the curtain of the rain. Slopes rose to the left; that should be north and west. "I think we must have gone eastward off the Gateham trail. That makes us already more than halfway to Shotton. We could reach Shotton by dark, and get to Gateham upstream along the burn in the morning."

"Are you sure? We've never been this way, either of us."

"Yes, I'm sure." Edmund, soaring above the earth like a lark as the abbot had taught him, could see it in his mind. Shotton was a smaller settlement, eastward and downstream from Gateham, where they had left the company the other day. "If we don't try it, we'll be in the hills overnight."

Derwin nodded reluctant agreement, and they set off. Derwin still lagged behind, and whenever Edmund looked back, he thought it looked like he was limping.

It was downhill, mostly, but the dark began to draw in as they reached a wooded area, the color of the autumn leaves fading with the light. *Saint Cuthbert, guide us!* thought Edmund as he gripped his pike, the memory of the wolf on Doddington Moor clear and sharp as yesterday. The light pike shaft with its small barbed tip had served often to spear a fish dinner when his travels took him near a burn, but he felt sure still that it would not be a match for Danes or wolves. But today, at least, they came through the trees without trouble. They hurried along the path, still barely visible and bending to their left.

"There! Derwin cried, and Edmund felt relief well up in him at the sight of firelight leaking out the half-open door of a house or small hall ahead. As they climbed the hill, Edmund could see the figure of a tall man, leaning on a spear and backlit by the inviting fire.

Edmund hailed him. "Travelers in need of hospitality!"

But the man's barked reply set his hair on end.

"Hverr ferr thar nu?"

chapter ten

ERWIN, FOLLOWING EDMUND, COLLIDED WITH HIM and cursed softly, and Riddle grumbled in complaint at being dislodged. Edmund cursed, too, silently—cursed *himself* for not approaching more cautiously. The man on guard before the hall spoke not English, but the language the invaders called the *Danske tunga.*

The warrior called out again, brandishing his spear while two more men emerged, one dark-haired with a torch, and the other a lean young man with fiery hair and a sword whose blade gleamed wickedly in the torchlight.

"Ed," Derwin said in a low voice, "You run—I'm half-lame now. You have to get to the bishop!"

"I'm not leaving you," Edmund growled. He kept hold of his fishing spear but was careful not to point it at the glaring Danes.

"*Beoth gesund,* Danes! Have you heard about your chief Half-dan? He's dead!"

The man with the sword stepped forward. He called sharply

to them, motioning to Edmund to put down the fishing spear. Edmund obeyed warily.

"If you aren't going, then I am!" said Derwin, and before Edmund could answer, he made a dash into the darkness of the trees to their left. Riddle took flight and soared above, cawing in alarm.

The Danes roared in anger, and as Edmund gaped into the night after his fleeing friend, a thrown spear whistled past him and thunked into flesh. Derwin screamed.

Edmund cried out, and Riddle's screams turned furious. The Danes uttered exclamations in their own language, most of which were nonsense to Edmund, but he recognized *hrafn*, raven.

"No!" Edmund lunged into the dark toward his friend and stumbled against his fallen form. "Derwin!" he cried, but got for answer only a terrible gasping. Then Edmund was yanked painfully back by the hair and thrown hard to the ground on his back. The dark-haired Dane with the torch planted his foot on Edmund's chest, forcing the air out of his lungs.

The red-haired man swung his blade, and it struck with a sound like a butcher's cleaver. Derwin's gasping halted instantly. Edmund had no breath to cry out, but hot tears sprang out the corners of his eyes. Through their wavering curtain he saw the wolfish grin of the copper-haired man as he leaned over to peer at Edmund. He barked orders at the others, who then dragged Edmund along the road and into the hall and threw him down.

"Get up!" said someone in front of him.

Edmund squinted his swollen eyes open. Before him on the raised dais, a Dane with a graying red beard and hair sat in a carved chair, which no doubt had once belonged to the English thegn of this little place. The dark-haired guardsman who had thrown his spear at Derwin stood to his left, the red-haired one who finished him with his sword to the right.

But it was a youth sitting at the Danish chief's feet who drew Edmund's gaze, for it was he who had spoken. Dark hair fell to the collar of a worn and faded blue tunic that had grown too short in the sleeves for him. The fine needlework trim was frayed. No jewelry. It all marked him as no one important—the youngest of many brothers, perhaps, or even a churl of no rank like Edmund himself, given the castoffs of his lord's son.

"On your feet before Jarl Thorstein," said the youth.

Bruised and aching, Edmund complied, raising his gaze to the man in the seat. The jarl's fading flame-colored locks and beard hung in elaborate braids, and his icy eyes fixed themselves on Edmund. He was leaning forward on the jeweled hilt of his drawn sword, and the light of hanging lamps and the hall's hearth fire flickered along its length, picking out the Danske rune letters marked on the blade.

"The Jarl wants your name and business here. Cause no trouble," the youth said, in an unfamiliar accent Edmund thought came from south of the Humber, "and you may keep your life, as your friend did not."

A flame of grief and hatred swelled up in Edmund, but before he could give in to the impulse to spit on the heathen letters on the sword, his blurred vision made of the weapon's hilt a cross, and the firelight and jewels seemed to him like blood. He heard Bishop Eardwulf's voice in his head repeating what he had said in many a homily on their travels, as they came to places that had lost folk to the invaders: *Vengeance is Mine, saith the Lord, I will repay.*

"Frana," said Thorstein, nodding to the red-haired man. Frana stepped forward, and the sudden sting of a leather belt cracked across Edmund's cheek, drawing a cry of pain from him.

Thorstein spoke gruffly in his own tongue, and the translator warned Edmund, "You had better answer now."

Edmund glared at him. "Why are you helping them? How did you learn the Danske tunga?"

The translator's eyebrows lifted in mild surprise. "I was born to it, English dog. It's *your* language I had to learn. Thorstein says, I killed the lord of Shotton yesterday, and it is mine now. I will have myself an English wife, I think. Would you know of a suitable lady?"

The men sniggered and Edmund gaped in astonishment.

"Where are you from?" the translator asked.

"Nowhere," said Edmund. "I've been wandering homeless these three years."

Thorstein's eyes narrowed suspiciously at the translation.

"Then who are you protecting?" asked the youth.

"No one. You killed the only friend I had," said Edmund, his voice dark.

"You're a bad liar," said the translator.

Edmund looked him in the eyes. "Because I'm not a traitor. Kill me now."

The translator did not smile or frown or smirk. His face was still and serious as he said, "But they won't kill you now. Thorstein was there when they killed your King Aelle at Jorvik, you know."

Edmund's stomach dropped. In his mind he was a small boy again, back in the dim fishing hut. Some neighbors had come to share drink and tales with his father. And one of them had told of Aelle and his brother, the two kings who each claimed Northumbria and fought each other—till the Danes came, and they had to join forces against the outland raiders. The leader of the Danes in those days was a jarl named Ivar, who killed Aelle and his brother at Eoforwic, which was what the translator meant by Jorvik.

"You know what they did to Aelle? The blood eagle?"

And then the translator did smirk, for he saw Edmund's fear.

Thorstein growled impatiently, and the translator spoke with him a little before turning to Edmund again.

Holy Cuthbert, help me stand firm, Edmund prayed silently. *O God—help me escape these evil men!*

Thorstein gave a little nod, and Frana cracked Edmund another blow with the belt, leaving him gasping.

Other men dragged him away and tied him to one of the hall-beams that supported the roof, facing away from the fire so he could hear the sounds of the people going about their work but could not see them.

The translator crouched in front of him.

"The blood eagle is a lie!" Edmund said. "A story made up to frighten people. King Aelle was killed in battle the same as his brother!"

The youth shrugged. "Are you sure?"

When Edmund only glared at him, he said, "Anyway, you'll be starved till you answer. And for what? I don't believe there are any English fighters left in this land. We are the jarls here, now."

"I'm not a traitor," Edmund said fiercely.

Something changed in the translator's expression, though Edmund could not quite say what. Then he looked away, got up and left.

Facing the timber wall, Edmund listened to the sounds of the hall behind his back—children crying, dogs growling, the clattering of wooden bowls and spoons. Some sort of steamy soup bubbled over the fire, and the savor of onions and leeks made his mouth water despite himself. He also discovered that being tied to a post was not just restraining, it quickly became painful. The Danes at their meal laughed and recited poems, and the laughter soon became wild with drink. But the Danske words were all a riddle to him, and Edmund fell at last into an exhausted doze.

When someone prodded him awake, the poems and laughter had given way to snoring, and the fire burned low. In the dim reddish glow he saw the translator lay a finger on his lips. Then he moved around behind Edmund and cut his bonds. Edmund struggled stiffly to his feet. Most of the hall folk were now sleeping in the curtained alcoves about the edges of the hall, except for a ragged boy with the shaven head of a slave, curled up with the dogs near the hearth. Edmund crept along in the translator's wake, hoping the rustle of rushes underfoot would not betray them.

A man who seemingly was supposed to be on guard lay sprawled and snoring before the threshold. They stepped around him and together lifted the bar of the double door, laying it softly down. The creaking hinges, the misty draft—Edmund's heart was in his mouth, expecting someone to rouse at any moment and raise the alarm. They slipped out and nudged the doors quietly closed behind them.

Then the translator sprinted across the yard, lit by full moonlight through the thinning mist, to a stable. Edmund was still hobbling after when the youth led out a tremendous red horse already saddled. He swung himself up, trotted the horse to a mounting block, and motioned for Edmund to clamber on behind. Edmund's muscles screamed complaint at him, but he managed, and soon they were slowly jogging down the road.

Some furlongs from the hall, the fog cleared entirely, and the youth goaded the horse into a faster pace. Edmund clung to his belt. A sword was slung across the translator's back, and the silver pommel cap glinted in the moonlight. As Edmund squirmed for a more comfortable position, his gaze focused on the small cross made of jet inlaid in the silver of the pommel. Sudden recognition dawned: Derwin's sword! Unthinking, he reached for the weapon, only to slide from his seat and land in the half-congealed mud of the road.

The horse cantered on a moment before the translator could turn it about again. "Have you never sat a horse before, Angle?"

"My name's Edmund!" he snapped, and then realized he had just freely given this youth the name he had refused, even on threat of torture, to surrender to Thorstein's men.

But the translator was uninterested. "Well, get back up!"

"Why are you helping me?" said Edmund.

The translator's face was impassive. "Don't look a gift horse in the mouth."

"Who are you—are you really a Dane?"

Edmund was unprepared for the sudden anger that blasted from the translator's eyes—like the hard wave of heat that would hit you in the face if you threw open the door of the blacksmith's shop. The youth jerked on the reins involuntarily, and the horse gave a whinny of protest. With visible effort he composed himself. "Who I am is none of your concern, prisoner. I am offering you your freedom, perhaps your very life."

Edmund folded his arms. "Do you think you can trick me into leading you to . . . to someone your jarl is looking for?"

The translator dismounted, took a breath and blew it out.

"I am escaping Thorstein's wretched band. If you do as I say, you too may escape."

"Why does a Dane need to escape from other Danes?" Edmund watched the translator's gestures, every tic and pull of the muscles of his face. "You aren't shorn like a slave, and you can't tell me you're even a churl. You ride like you were born to it."

The translator did not answer at once, but then he said, "A fatherless boy can remain free in name but not truth, if his father's friends turn out to be friends only in name and not truth."

Don't trust him, Edmund warned himself, for his heart went out to the teller of such a cruel tale. Still, the youth held himself very closely, and gave no sign of pleading for sympathy. "And how does it benefit you to help me?"

The translator's mouth turned up at one edge, a little as Bishop Eardwulf's often did. "You will remember that the son of Harthacnut helped you. And tell that to . . . whoever it is you aren't betraying."

Edmund stood in doubt for a moment. Could he trust him? Did he have any choice? But then he remembered the terrible sound of the spear going home, and Derwin's scream, and the fatal blow of the sword . . .

"No! You're one of them—those filthy Danes who killed Derwin! And you've taken Derwin's sword!" Edmund cried, and in sudden fury flung himself at the other youth.

They scrabbled on the ground for a moment, but Edmund's injuries told, and he found himself lying in the road. The translator stood over him—loomed like a warrior now, the sword drawn and laid against Edmund's throat. "They gave it me, for translating. It's a terrible sword," the youth said calmly, "badly made, badly balanced. But it will do the job." After a moment to let that sink in, he stepped away from Edmund and sheathed the weapon, then remounted his horse. "If you hope to live, my advice is to leave the road. Be careful of your tracks in the mud."

He wheeled the horse, about to move on.

"Wait!" Edmund scrambled to his feet, and the translator paused expectantly.

"I thank you for my life and freedom," Edmund said, a little stiffly.

The youth shrugged. "You now bear a debt of honor, Angle. If you have honor, then you don't need to thank me. Just flee." He turned and urged the horse into a trot westward, toward the river ford on the north side of the road.

Edmund left the road at once on the south side, avoiding soft spots that would make his prints stand out amongst the rest, and struggled through the woods, up the hills, and finally back to the place where he and Derwin first realized they had lost their way the other day. There, like the people by the waters of Babylon in the psalm, he sat down and wept. And it was there that Riddle finally found him again.

chapter eleven

RIDDLE CAME AND WENT AS EDMUND TOILED THROUGH the hills to the path they should have taken the day before. He dragged himself back into Gateham late in the day, faint from hunger and thirst.

The monks sang a memorial for Derwin in the small church of Gateham. Derwin's father, Stitheard the gruff and brave, fell weeping on Edmund's neck. Over on the women's side, Edmund could see Aelfleda sobbing, and he glimpsed Caris too. Her face, framed by its linen veil, was blank and still as one of the standing stones of Doddington moor.

When the service ended, the people hurried out, and the monks filed after, singing. Edmund then begged a favor of the bishop: "Let me keep vigil by Saint Cuthbert's body alone tonight."

"If Stitheard agrees," said the bishop, and Stitheard, his eyes hollow, said, "Yes. I want work. We pack up tonight?"

"We do," said the bishop. "I hoped the company could winter here, but this Thorstein is too close for comfort at Shotton.

Gateham is likely too big for him to take and hold with the few men Edmund saw, but Gateham hasn't enough warriors to protect our company either." He and the bearers went out then, leaving Edmund to kneel in the silence before the coffin, candles alight at each side. Derwin's body was not here—Edmund feared Thorstein might even have given it to the dogs—but Cuthbert's body was here, and here Edmund would watch to honor his friend.

Yet he found that all he could think of was Derwin's sword—and Thorstein's, and Frana's. Phrases from poems seemed to pop around his head, about sharp swords slaking thirst, metal tongues drinking deep, blades bedewed with blood.

"*Kyrie eleison,*" Edmund breathed, for it was all the prayer he had strength for.

The sound of the door creaking cracked his half-dream open to reality, and he snapped alert, jumping to his feet. Abbot Eadred slipped in through the opening, making the sign of the cross.

He came and gave Edmund a pat on the shoulder, then turned to a table that was set to one side of the holy coffin. There was kept the other great treasure the company had carried with them. "Edmund, have you ever seen the great Gospel book of Lindesfarne?"

"Me? No! I mean, only the cover when the bishop brings it out in church on high feast days."

"Come and I will show you."

Eadred lifted the box lid and stood it on end against the table, and Edmund crossed himself as the uncovered gold and jewels flashed in the candlelight. This was one of the great treasures the Danes so coveted, but they did not understand its true value. Eadred lifted the Gospel out of the box to hold it out before him, and Edmund, trembling, placed a reverent kiss upon a large pearl at the center of the cross that adorned the cover. Then Edmund removed the box from the table so that the abbot could lay the holy book on the surface, release the bronze latches on the sides, and open it up.

Edmund felt he had stepped into a dream. Or a poem. He gazed in silence as Abbot Eadred slowly leafed through the book, revealing the intricate forms and glowing colors that adorned the pages of the Gospels—the holiest of Scripture, telling the life of the Lord Jesus Christ Himself, His death on the Cross, and His Resurrection from the dead. Edmund knew every church and monastery had books of Scripture and read from one of the Gospels at every mass, just as the company of Cuthbert did. But this special and wonderful copy was made more than a hundred years ago by a bishop-artist of Lindesfarne, as an offering of art and love to God and Saint Cuthbert.

He recognized the portraits of the four Gospel-writers, and with difficulty he could read some of the Latin letters; but what drew him most were the pages that showed drawings of the cross. The inks of brilliant red, gold, blue, green, and black formed dense patterns, like finely woven cloth. When you looked closer you would see sometimes animals and birds with limbs looped and twined about each other in dizzying spirals.

Edmund felt he was drawn in somehow to the deep workings of Creation. All these tiny figures, connected to each other, were like a great chorus of creatures singing the praise of the Creator, and every drop of colored ink like a musical tone. The Gospel book brimmed full of a great teeming mysterious dance that was yet the calmest, stillest thing he had ever seen.

Eadred closed the book again and put it away. "God be with you," he said to Edmund, and left him alone with Cuthbert again.

In the morning he was summoned to see the bishop in the little common hut borrowed from the secular clerks that kept the church here at Gateham.

"I brought you here to ask if you are well enough to serve me again. In a new position."

Edmund was speechless. And then hopeful. Was he at last to be allowed a horse and learn the long-distance ways from Brother Aethelbert, who had taken over from the much-missed Herebert?

He gulped air and said, "Yes, my lord bishop!"

"Raedwulf has taken ill, and he must stay here. We must have another layman to join the bearers of Saint Cuthbert. Stitheard and I are agreed it should be you."

Edmund gaped. "A saint-bearer? Me? But I'm a runner! And a fisherman—don't you need a cartwright or a herdsman?"

"Stitheard will teach you anything necessary. He would have you because you were his son's friend. But more, Abbot Eadred tells me he sees some special bond between you and our holy father Cuthbert. Cuthbert himself wants you."

"But I thought—I hoped I might be taught to ride now, and bear messages further afield!"

The bishop's brows rose, a smile touching his lips, but when he said nothing, Edmund sputtered, "And . . . and there's my mother and sister," he added. "My mother has only me for a man in the family, since Hunred is one of the bearers already!"

This time the bishop actually chuckled. "Edmund, when you came into Gateham yesterday so bloody and bedraggled, bringing the news about Derwin, your mother was the first to beg that I provide you some duty less dangerous, that would keep you in the company."

Edmund felt like a stunned fish that had been slammed down on the boards of a fishing boat. *This is my punishment for losing Derwin*, he thought. *As if losing him weren't punishment enough in itself!*

But the bishop spoke not of punishment. "To bear the saint, Edmund—how few are chosen for this task!"

Edmund closed his eyes. It was like trying to catch the wind in your sails when the direction kept changing, and you lurched back and forth between the sail and the tiller to try to steer because you were alone in the boat . . . *because your father had been washed overboard in the storm . . .*

His eyes snapped open, and he gasped at the sudden surfacing of the long-buried memory. *I called on Cuthbert that day, and I don't know how I ever got home alone in the boat . . . the wind changed and drove the boat back into Lindesfarne harbor . . .*

The bishop was looking at him intently. And Edmund couldn't speak, but he slowly nodded his head.

"*Deo gratias,*" said Eardwulf. He stood and signed the cross over Edmund, and Edmund kissed his ring. "Fetch your things from your family and come to the church."

Edmund ran to obey. Only when he stood before the church door did he remember: As one of the bearers, he would now spend the bulk of the day, every day, in the company of his brother Hunred.

EDMUND PLODDED ALONG IN HIS PLACE AT THE FRONT RIGHT corner of the cart. They had only traveled from the church to the riverside to join with the layfolk, and already the maddening slowness of ox-pace was numbing Edmund's soul. The rain eased to mist, which was just as cold and wet. Riddle sat dejectedly on his shoulder, making a sad clicking noise in Edmund's ear.

Suddenly Edmund caught the distant rumble of many hoof-beats behind them. "Listen!" he blurted, and the rest of the company turned too, peering into the fog veiling the road that had brought them here from Gateham church.

It only took a few moments for Thorstein and his grinning men to emerge from the mist and spread themselves out around the cart and bearers, between them and the rest of the company. Edmund pulled his hood down low over his face lest he be recognized.

Shrieks rose from the women, and the farmers and fishermen groaned even as they stepped forward with their pitiful array of weapons—walking sticks, hoes, a few knives and fishing pikes. The monks turned pale and crossed themselves, muttering *misereres*. Thorstein sat regally on his mount while Frana came forward and pranced his horse around, ogling the women and exchanging what sounded like contemptuous remarks with the other Danes. There were fifteen of them on their horses, their swords still sheathed but their ring mail gleaming.

The translator was not with them, and despite himself Edmund was glad the youth had escaped them. At least, he supposed so . . . it might be Thorstein had caught him and punished him . . .

"Put your weapons away," Eardwulf called to the laymen. "You are no match for these warriors."

"We outnumber them!" cried one of the hall-men, who brandished a spear.

"Do as the bishop says!" Stitheard bellowed, and the men reluctantly stood down.

Thorstein nodded in condescending approval. His eye rested on Aelfleda, mounted on her donkey amongst the other women, appraising the evidence of her worn but fine gown and veil, and the intricate bronze pin that held her cloak. A woman of some standing, the Dane had to know. He called and beckoned.

"Let her be, in God's name!" To Edmund's astonishment, the shouted protest came from none other than Hunred, who beyond all belief started away from his holy post beside the coffin.

The Dane jarl's head swung round, his brows thunderous, and Stitheard barked at Hunred, "Back to your place, man!" But Stitheard himself watched his daughter with frightening intensity.

Edmund devoutly wished the translator back again. But when Aelfleda, pale and trembling, dismounted with the help of another woman and hobbled toward him, Thorstein wrinkled his nose in dissatisfaction. He pointed to the bronze pin, and she undid it and handed it to him.

Meanwhile, Frana turned his gaze instead on Brother Aethelbert's horse. A gesture from Frana, and the monk had to hand over the reins.

The warriors went amongst the layfolk, snatching up a few chickens or sacks of grain. And then the red-haired Frana heaved a girl screaming over his shoulder. Merewyn! "No!" cried Edmund.

"Steady!" the bishop said grimly. "Wait!" He stepped forward and hailed the jarl. Thorstein grinned, and Edmund's stomach dropped. *He's playing with us*, he thought, *he was just waiting for the bishop to offer something . . .*

"The purse, Brother Wilfred."

The purser, pale-faced, came forward with the pouch of coins. Thorstein took it, peered in, and affected to be disgusted with the contents. But he tied it to his belt anyway. Then he dared to make for the cart and its holy burden.

People gasped, and the monks closed ranks around the bearers. But then Riddle rose screaming into the air and swooped toward the Dane jarl, who stepped back in startlement.

Exclamations of "Hrafn!" escaped the warriors, and other short, sharp words that Edmund was sure were curses. Riddle circled about their heads, scolding, while everyone watched. Then down he came again and landed on Cuthbert's coffin.

A beat or two of silence, and Eardwulf pointed to Frana, still holding the sobbing Merewyn, and said, "Give the girl back to her mother."

Thorstein peered with narrowed eyes at the raven on the coffin, but then inclined his head to Frana, who put Merewyn down. She ran to her mother, who gratefully clutched her close.

And Abbot Eadred began to chant. *Iam lucis* it was again, like that day on the moor, though it was well past the right time for the morning hymn. And the monks joined in, and then everyone who knew even a little of it. "*Nos servet a nocentibus,*" Edmund chimed in, still huddling in his cloak. *Preserve us from all harm!*

The Danes looked at each other. Thorstein gave the bishop a poisonous look, then spat on the ground. *Saving face and pretending we're not worth it,* Edmund guessed, as the jarl wheeled his horse around. Before the hymn was over, he and his men had galloped away into the mist, leaving only a distant and receding sound of hoofbeats.

THE COMPANY MADE CAMP AT A ROMAN RUIN IN THE KALE valley that night, with a sailcloth tent rigged over the coffin of the saint. The monks and people huddled against various half-fallen walls under whatever shelter they could manage to make. Once the tent was safely erected, Stitheard gathered the other six bearers to make their own camp a little way distant, leaving the monks to carry on with services at the appointed hours of the night.

"Hunred," said Stitheard, "Take Edmund and show him how we look after Lindo for the night."

The glum ox perked its ears and gave out a little low that sounded almost cheerful when Hunred led him away toward the far end of the camp, where the animals sheltered by the one tree in sight, a twisted hawthorn. To Edmund's surprise, Riddle swooped in from the sky to perch on Lindo's shoulder, bird and ox alike acting as if it were a familiar routine.

The man tending the company's other ox, which pulled the largest supply cart, greeted them with a nod. Hunred took some oats from a sack and fed them to Lindo, and Edmund followed his example, allowing Riddle a share as well. When the cart animal had eaten several handfuls, Hunred said, "That's enough, now we let him graze a little. Come, Lindesfarne," he said, with a little whistle, and the ox followed obediently.

They had given a very small amount of the good feed to the hard-working animal. But the goats and donkeys got none, contenting themselves with vetch and grasses on the slopes of the hill. If even the holy ox that drew the saint's coffin-cart was now allowed so few oats after a full day's work, what would happen to all the company's people in winter?

"Now while he grazes, we have a good look in all directions," said Hunred. "Abbot Eadred says open your eyes, your ears, your nose, and your thoughts, and if—"

"If there is anything to be learned, we will learn it. We do the same on messenger duty," said Edmund. "I'll take west and north," he said, and promptly turned to make the survey, though a lump stuck in his throat. *We* used to be Edmund and Derwin, and if he had remembered the abbot's training, it might be Edmund and Derwin still.

chapter twelve

IN THE VALLEYS TO THE SOUTH, THE HARVEST WOULD be falling under the sickle even now. But the high Cheviots could be brutally unpredictable and cruel to travelers. Before the next day was out, an early snow squall caught the company like a school of fishes unable to escape the tangled net of lonely sheep tracks in the south of the hills. The wind drove wet snow down on them from the hilltops, and they huddled into cloaks, struggling head down along the muddy road, hardly able to see where they were going. Edmund, positioned ahead of the wheel, wished he were behind Brother Aidan's sheltering bulk instead. Riddle hunched in the lee of the Saint's coffin atop the box holding the great Gospel book, and no one rebuked him.

A man came back to see Stitheard, shouting over the wind, "We've lost half the goats! They heard some wild 'uns baaing at 'em and off they went."

A most unholy curse burst from Stitheard. The bishop did not rebuke him, but said to the other man, "Leave them to

God. Tell me, what can you see ahead? Have our runners come back yet?"

"That they have not, my lord bishop," said the man, clumps of ice beads falling off his hood as he shook his head.

"Just keep on, then!"

The goatherd had barely left when Stitheard said to the bishop, "So we *have* missed our turn!" The tone of accusation and the clear revelation of an ongoing argument shocked Edmund.

Eardwulf's reply was tight. "We will keep on. *If* we have missed the turn, the runners will come to find us."

Stitheard gave a dissatisfied growl for answer, but plodded on, patting the miserable ox's neck. The bearers slipped now and then in the cold mud. Before long the hills began to darken. Someone else, a boy, came running back from the front of the column again—Cuthwin, the smith's boy, Edmund realized, whom Edmund had once knocked down by running without looking. *Now he's the age I was when this all started. And if things go on this way much longer, will he ever get to be much older—will any of us?*

"My lord bishop," said Cuthwin, "there's a shepherd's botl ahead. No other shelter but some lambing sheds."

"Let the aged and mothers with little ones go in, if there be room enough. Cuthbert will stay on the cart, and the monks gather round him. The rest must make shift as best they can."

So they trudged on to the shepherd's place, where they drew the wagons and barrows in a circle about the stone wall of the botl. The shepherd himself regarded them with dismay bordering on animosity.

"I beg your forgiveness, friend," said Eardwulf, "but the Danes took our purse as we left Gateham. We will recompense you however we can before we go."

"Little good that will do me when Lord Osbert's reeve asks me to account for the animals!" the man spat.

"We have not asked for any sheep," said the bishop, growing impatient.

But Stitheard broke in, "Leash your tongue when you speak to God's holy bishop, you thick-headed stump! Anyway, the lord at Aelfsdene owes the bishop *years'* worth of stock! Be thankful to God that He has sent you a holy company bearing the body of a saint, and not a pack of Danes to kill you and take the whole flock!"

"Oh, *that* for *God!*" sneered the shepherd, and spat on the ground. "No need of Danes here, God already sent a pack of *wolves* to take most of this year's lambs, He did!"

Edmund could not help letting out a gasp at this impiety, and he heard the same from one or two of the other bearers.

But Stitheard waved it away. "Complain to God, then! I will not see these people starve and freeze. We are not asking. We are taking!"

"*Stitheard.*" The bishop's voice was the stern and quiet one that Edmund had learned was a sign of true anger, but Stitheard ignored him and hallooed to some of the men of the company. "Get ropes and knives! It's mutton for supper!" He turned again to the shepherd. "You'd best call any dogs you have to heel. If they give my men any trouble, we won't spare them."

"If I had dogs, don't you think they'd have warned you off when you got here?" said the shepherd. "I told you, the wolves are bad this year. My last dog went down fighting them yesterday." For the first time there was a break in his voice. "And now this early storm—and on top of all, *you* lot come marching in!"

They all stood in embarrassed silence for a moment, as the fury in the man's eyes turned to tears of grief and frustration.

And then Eardwulf threw himself in the mud at the shepherd's feet. "In the name of God and Saint Cuthbert, man, I beg you to forgive us! My monks and I will not touch the mutton, we will eat the cheese and dried fish we carry with us. But you see all the women and little children and old folk with us, and the men bearing heavy burdens on the road. We are exiles and pilgrims all, we come to you as the angels came to receive hospitality from the patriarch Abraham."

Edmund had to look away, watching instead the laymen and monks setting up shelters of sorts between the botl and the lambing sheds. But he could not close his ears to the shepherd's sob.

Abruptly, Stitheard said, "Franco, Hunred, Edmund—come with me, my boys, and we'll raise the canopy and build a fire."

Edmund followed, a feeling of dread in his stomach. He could see the crack appearing in the company—Stitheard had left the three bearers who were monks with the bishop and their reluctant host, and taken the lay bearers—and the novice Franco—with him.

The chore of raising the canopy nearly froze their fingers, but Edmund felt a tiny lift in his heart when the shepherd came to them with a load of firewood. Too shamefaced to look them in the eye, but Edmund called out thanks as the man made for his botl again.

It was the worst night yet since they left Lindesfarne. The hall men, working together, slaughtered and butchered several sheep efficiently. Cooking was less efficient, the first joints sent into the botl for the women and children, and only the one outdoor fire by the botl's stone wall struggling against the wind to cook the rest on long sticks. The butchers got first chance at that, while the rest waited their turn. The monks meanwhile sang vespers, despite the wind and cold and sleet, with no shelter but their cloaks as they gathered close together around the coffin-cart.

"Someone should be keeping wolf-watch," Edmund worried aloud, while he and the other bearers waited their turn to skewer some mutton and char it over the struggling flames.

"If the wolves get another sheep in this weather, welcome to it," said Stitheard.

"Stitheard?" Franco, the red-haired novice, spoke for the first time since their arrival. "Have I leave to go back to the monks now? I—I can't eat the meat." He gave the sizzling morsels over the fire a longing look.

Stitheard regarded him for a moment. "You're only a novice. And anyway, hardly any of the monks go without meat all the time."

"Abbot Eadred keeps the old customs," Hunred said, though no one had asked his opinion. "And the bishop always did too, until our journey."

Stitheard ignored him, fixing his gaze on Franco. "Half-monk, half-not, you were supposed to be the balance beam. But it's really been monks first all along, hasn't it?"

Franco looked down. If his fair cheeks had not already been scoured red by the cold and wind, Edmund was sure they would have colored with emotion. *Balance beam!* What a terrible weight to lay on poor Franco, who was always a meek and timid sort.

"Go on," sighed Stitheard, and Franco lost no time obeying.

And that left Edmund and Hunred.

"With your permission, Stitheard," said Hunred, "I too would prefer to go and share the monks' meal."

"*You* are definitely *not* a monk!" piped Edmund. It was the first time he had even spoken to Hunred all day.

"My heart is a monk's heart," said Hunred.

"The bishop doesn't think so, or you would be one by now!"

"Edmund," Stitheard warned.

Hunred bit his lip and waited for the head bearer's answer.

"Well, then," said Stitheard, "Go eat with the monks. More mutton for you and me, Edmund."

OVERNIGHT, THE SNOW AND SLEET TURNED TO RAIN, AND the next morning, under a clearing sky, the shepherd joined the company long enough to set them on their way. Aelfsdene, he assured them, was in easy reach today, "and the road there mostly downhill, too!" Best of all, it was definitely free of Danish occupation.

"A band of them came through the Rede Valley a year ago, and young Lord Osbert fought them to a standstill," the shepherd said with a touch of pride.

About noon, when they had left the heights well behind, the messengers caught them up from behind—it was they and not the company, it turned out, who had lost their way. Downcast and hungry, the men were given a little bread and dry fish. Eardwulf chose a new pair to go as herald before the company to Aelfsdene.

Today Stitheard set Edmund to walk beside the ox, to accustom him to the use of the switch to gently guide the animal. As the bearers prepared to move on from their brief halt, Caris turned up, begging a word with the bishop.

Edmund was shocked at the hollow look of her eyes, and wondered if his own were as dim and hurt.

"My lord bishop, we are making for Aelfsdene?"

"As I told everyone before we set out from Gateham, Caris." To Edmund the edge in Eardwulf's voice warned that his patience, like the cloak he had worn for three winters, was wearing thin. "What's on your mind?"

"Your promise to me, my lord bishop."

She may be weary and battered about the heart, thought Edmund, smiling in admiring amusement, *but she never quits throwing her net back in the water.*

Eardwulf did not break stride. "I have not forgotten my promise, nor have I forgotten that you are now of age."

"Only we are going to Aelfsdene."

"And perhaps you will change your mind when you get there."

"I will not! Never!"

"Even though the reasons you left are now gone?"

This struck Caris silent, and after a moment she kissed the bishop's hand and turned to go back to her place among the layfolk at the front of the column. But then, to Edmund's surprise, Riddle gave a loud "Cronk!" and left his place on Edmund's shoulder to perch instead on Caris's.

"La! Riddle! Come back!" he shouted, and gave a piercing whistle.

Brought up short, Caris almost smiled as she stroked the bird's breast feathers. Almost. Her face was unreadable as she shrugged and said to Edmund, "He goes where he wants, when he wants. He'll come back to you. He always did to Derwin."

However, instead of heading back to the layfolk in the front of the column, Caris continued to walk in front of the bearers, behind the monks.

The track narrowed and paralleled a little burn on their right, while oaks and elms tinged with autumn color now covered the slopes to their left. When they cleared the woods, Edmund could see the straggling column of travelers ahead wending its way past fields of oats and barley. The sun beamed above, and under their feet the road was actually dusty, the whole valley untouched by the storm clouds that had attacked the company with snow and sleet in the high hills only yesterday. In fact, it was perfect harvest weather—and that was what was happening up ahead. The leading foot travelers of the company had come to a halt in a bunch at the far edge of the field and were talking with the Aelfsdene folk at work in the fields. A fair-haired man on a black horse detached himself from the group and came towards them.

The bishop raised his voice. "Bearers and monks of Saint Cuthbert, halt!"

"Haul back, boys!" Stitheard cried to the bearers. "Edmund—stop him like I showed you!"

The ox, he meant. It was alarming to be faced with those horns, but Lindo would not stop unless you planted yourself firmly in front of him and placed your hand on his head. Edmund had never wanted so badly to be a fisherman again . . .

The bearers cried "Whoa!" as they heaved backward on the cart frame and ropes holding the saint's coffin on. The ox cart slowed, creaking mightily, and Edmund's open palm came to rest gently on the warm hide of the animal's forehead. With a grunt and a snuffle, Lindesfarne came to a stop and stood chewing cud and switching his tail.

"Beoth gesund, haliwerfolc!"

Edmund looked over his shoulder to see the rider dismounting. He was barely bearded, only a few years older than Edmund, and his pale red-gold hair escaped from its braids in thin straight strands in the breeze. Though he carried no sword at the moment, fine trappings on the horse-gear and the glint of gold on his arms proclaimed him the Lord Osbert the shepherd had praised. Once more Edmund felt the knife of envy in his soul. Not that he wanted gold, or to tell other people what to do . . . but oh, the horse, the beautiful black horse with its rippling muscles, the horse that was freedom to go anywhere, and above all to go quickly!

The young thegn knelt for the bishop's blessing—that was a better start than last night's welcome from the shepherd, at least. And then something strange happened. While young Osbert, lord of Aelfsdene, was inviting the company to join the harvest work and the feast to follow, Edmund gazed past the young lord's shoulder at the crowd of monks who had turned to watch as well. There alone of the layfolk stood Caris, Riddle still on her shoulder, her face pale as the snow they had left behind in the hills. Wisps of hair straggled out the veil-edge around her face, and her eyes, reflecting the blue of the sky, had gone round as cups beneath her straight brows.

And there, closer before him, Edmund saw on the face of Thegn Osbert the same blue eyes, the same straight brows and pale red-gold hair, a face in a more manly cast but still, unmistakably, the badge of a shared family written in Caris's features.

chapter thirteen

IDDLE PIPED UP SUDDENLY WITH ONE OF HIS RAU-
cous attention-getting calls, drawing Osbert's gaze.
Most people—apart from Thorstein's men—reacted
with surprise and delight on first seeing the tame raven, but
Osbert instantly focused on the young woman whose shoulder
provided the raven a perch.

"Caris?" The astonished exclamation burst from him.

Edmund had never seen Caris so utterly at bay. She stared at
the ground, spots of color flaring high on her cheekbones.

"Lord Osbert," said the bishop, "let this be now, and you and
I will speak tonight. Caris, go back to the other womenfolk."

Caris gave her head a little jerky nod and scuttled away without kissing the bishop's hand. Osbert stared after her till she
passed out of view beyond the gathered monks.

"Tell me, Osbert," the bishop said pointedly, "is there now a
church at Aelfsdene, as your father once promised me?"

Osbert turned again and shook his head glumly. "No, my lord
bishop, I am sorry. The Danes . . ."

He turned his palms up in a gesture of despair.

"I see."

Edmund knew how Osbert felt under Eardwulf's sharp eyes. The silence stretched until the young thegn looked up quickly.

"But I promise," he said, "when the Danes are defeated, I will build a church for Saint Cuthbert here!"

"Suppose the Danes are *not* defeated?"

The words went like a cold wave over the monks and bearers, and Edmund felt it in himself too. No such fearful words had ever been uttered by anyone in the company—till now.

"I know their leader Halfdan is dead," said Eardwulf. "But the other Danes have settled south of Tyne for good. They have sent for their women and children, and moved into the halls belonging to the English lords they killed in battle. Most of them are wise enough not to mistreat the English churls on the estates, and so it is that Danish jarls are called lords in Northumbria."

Osbert drew himself up proudly. "They did not take the Rede Valley here! I and my men thrashed them at Bellingham to the south. What few of them survived scattered about and do us no more harm."

"No harm!" Edmund's mouth seemed to open of its own accord. "A jarl named Thorstein killed my friend at Shotton. His men took the company's purse from the bishop himself, bold as you please!"

"Edmund." The bishop laid a hand on his arm.

Osbert stared at him. "Who is this young churl?"

"He is neither churl nor thegn nor slave nor anything else save a holy servant of Saint Cuthbert, as are all these men you see here—monk and layman alike, they are set apart to tend and guard the relics of the saint on this cart."

Osbert's expression changed instantly. "Saint Cuthbert?

Himself?" Trembling and wide-eyed, the young thegn made the sign of the cross and fell to his knees before the ox cart. Edmund heard Stitheard give a little grunt of satisfaction.

"On your feet now, Osbert," said the bishop, his voice kindly now as Edmund had often known it to turn after sternness. "When your harvest is in, we will speak of it."

OSBERT GALLOPED AWAY, AND THE BEARERS PLODDED ON toward the hall. They passed harvest workers on their left, including many of the company's own men who had joined the Aelfsdene folk already. Children were busily scaring birds from the grain, Riddle among them. When a boy took a swipe at him with a switch, he flew to Edmund's shoulder again, and Edmund smiled at the dismay on the boy's face when Riddle sat there safe and scolded him vigorously. Into a grassy pasture to the right, the company's wagons and animals were brought, and there camp was set up.

Abbot Eadred and a few monks came to chant the evening office. Edmund stood with the other bearers, and the litanies carried him like a wave back to Lindesfarne. He closed his eyes and prayed with all his might, *Let us go back to Lindesfarne. Let us go home again! Soon. Soon. Soon.*

Then it was done and Abbot Eadred said, "Osbert has invited the bearers to his table, but the bishop and I agree it is not fitting for monks. He must go for politeness, but I will stay here with the monks and watch by Cuthbert. You as well, Franco. We will take our supper from our packs."

Stitheard grunted in approval. "Hunred, Edmund—I was also told by the bishop that you now have leave to go and see your mother. But go to the rain barrel by the hall and wash and comb your hair first!"

"Yes, Stitheard!" said Edmund, and sprinted away down the hill toward the hall yard. At first it was just to get away from Hunred, but within a few steps the joy of running caught him, and he kept on running, past the hall and out along the road.

He ran past the workers in the fields, nearly as far as the trees again, only pausing reluctantly because the sun was lowering, and he knew he had to go and pay respects to his mother before the harvest feast began at sunset. Panting and sweating, he made his way from the road past the brush to the sparkling burn, only to pull up short when he saw Caris and Osbert talking in the shade of the willows, while the black horse nibbled on the plants at water's edge.

They were too engrossed to notice him, so he was only a stone's throw away when Osbert said, "But Caris. People want to make alliances with me now—even people in Mercia and Wessex. Times are too troubled for them to worry overmuch about niceties. If I give you one of my estates and call you my sister, as you are, no one in those far places will think to ask whether your mother happened to be a Wealisc slave. I'll get you a better match than any Bishop Eardwulf could find you!"

Caris's jaw dropped, and Edmund instantly knew what was coming, though the slap on the cheek caught Osbert utterly off guard. Caris spun on her heel and tramped toward the road.

"Edmund, what are you doing here?" she flung at him crossly as she passed, and kept going without waiting for an answer. For his part, Edmund was transfixed by Osbert's gobsmacked stare. Wild laughter welled up in him, and he could not tamp it back down. Osbert's attention went from Caris to Edmund. Even the black horse stopped nibbling and raised an inquisitive head.

Finally Edmund shook his head and said, "Are you stupid? Do you even know her? You just insulted her mother and her betrothed in the same breath!" Suddenly the tide of laughter in him turned, and his next words came out as sobs. "Her betrothed was my friend Derwin that the Danes killed at Shotton—just days ago!"

Comprehension filled the young thegn's face. He gave a heavy sigh and then sat down by the waterside, closing his eyes.

Edmund, his sobs easing, went to the burn to wash his face and comb his hair.

"You're right," said Osbert. "I should have known. She hasn't changed. I'm only trying to make up for how it was for her when we grew up here . . ."

Edmund came back and sat by Osbert. "She's really your sister? She says her mother was a Wealisc king's daughter."

"Almost. Say lord, or whatever the Wealas call a thegn, instead of king. And say granddaughter, or maybe great-granddaughter instead of daughter." He scrabbled among the pebbles on the bank and tossed a few into a smooth-surfaced pool midstream. They plopped in, making circles that vanished quickly.

Riddle wheeled overhead, scolding, as if to nag Edmund about getting back to his mother. Edmund whistled the bird down, to Osbert's admiration.

"Is it you he belongs to, or Caris? I saw him on her shoulder today—"

"He was Derwin's," said Edmund, his heart aching and his voice thick. After an awkward moment, he said, "You didn't finish telling me about growing up with Caris."

Osbert looked thoughtfully out at the burn for a moment before his eyes met Edmund's again. "Yes, she is my sister. But my mother was a lady, and hers a Wealisc slave."

"So that makes Caris a slave too."

Osbert shook his head. "No. She is a thegn's daughter. The law says a thegn has to free any children he has by a slave. He doesn't have to give them thegn status or property or any inheritance, but he has to free them. Except my father never freed Caris. Because . . ." Osbert looked away. "Because my mother begrudged it." A little defensively he added, "As would any lady to her husband's child by a slave."

Don't criticize his family, Edmund told himself, biting his tongue hard, but Osbert's story filled him with outrage. The first time the company had stayed at a secular estate, he had learned about men and women who did not keep to their lawful wedded mates, and the unhappy children who resulted. The boys at that hall had mocked all the Lindesfarne children for their innocence. Still Edmund believed the way people lived on Lindesfarne in the shelter of the monastery was best, one man and one wife, and children obedient to their elders . . . well, *mostly* obedient, he admitted to himself . . .

"And then my father died," said Osbert. "And with Danes attacking, and no moots being held for law judgments . . . no one did anything about Caris, till she was old enough to understand, and called on Bishop Eardwulf for help. He took her away."

He sighed then, and changed the subject. "Come. I have not heard any tales of Saint Cuthbert since I was a boy. You must know many of them!"

Edmund stood up. "I must beg your pardon—I have to go pay my respects to my mother before the feast. But if you want to hear stories of Cuthbert, ask for Reeve Stitheard's daughter Aelfleda."

To Edmund's relief, when he found his mother and Merewyn in the camp set up in the pasture, he got no scolding for his delay but only a great deal of fuss and a clean tunic. The weather still held fine, so sailcloth had been spread on the ground to rest upon rather than propped up for shelter with poles.

Hunred sat cross-legged and silent, also wearing a spare tunic their mother had kept for him amongst her luggage. Merewyn, having hugged Edmund thoroughly, now went back to sewing a repair patch on another part of the cloth. It was far from the only tear in the woolen fabric, Edmund noticed.

He looked at Merewyn's face and didn't like its thinness as she sat concentrating on her needlework. Osbert was determined to help his sister and give her a whole estate if he could, even though they had two different mothers. But what could Edmund do for Merewyn? It had to be Edmund; Hunred had his head in the clouds and wouldn't even think of the need.

Up the road at the hall, the clanging of a hammer against an iron bar sounded—substitute for a bell on this churchless estate, Edmund supposed.

The family walked up to the hall together with other company members. The aroma of roasting meat from cookfires in the yard wafted toward them, and the Aelfsdene churls stood with cups in hand around the barrels of beer. Hunred and Edmund bade the distaff side of the family good evening and approached the open door of the hall. Osbert's reeve, a graybeard with a game leg and eye patch, greeted them and, leaning on his staff, led them to a table just before the platform upon which stood the lord's table. Stitheard and the bishop were already seated there with Osbert, some other well-dressed young men, and one older lady Edmund imagined must be a relative of Osbert's.

All so young, Edmund thought of the men. *Their fathers probably died fighting the Danes too.*

"Waes hal, Hunred. Waes hal, Edmund." Across the table from them, Aelfleda's smile beamed. And the rest of her shone too.

"You look like a reeve's daughter again!" Edmund blurted, and Aelfleda pinkened with pleasure.

"Thegn Osbert's aunt gave me this new veil—the finest linen I ever owned! Gave it to me! The headband I brought from home with me, it was my mother's," she said, touching the faded red ribbon with little silver rings sewn on that secured the veil. "And the gown Osbert's aunt has lent me till my own is washed and mended. Look, feel how soft the wool is!" she enthused, extending her arm across the table toward Hunred.

He looked so uncomfortable that Edmund could barely stifle a laugh. Hunred took the edge of the wide green sleeve between thumb and forefinger, nodded and muttered, "Very fine."

Aelfleda said, "Did you hear Lord Osbert has promised to build a church? And he will see the company hosted at all his other estates when we leave here!"

"It's easy to promise," said Hunred.

The edge in his voice made Edmund glance sideways at him in surprise. Unflappable Hunred, upset about . . . about what, exactly?

Osbert's reeve boomed out a call to order. The crowded tables about the hall fell silent, and the laughter and shouting of the estate churls drifted in from the yard as the bishop stood to intone the blessing on the meal.

Fresh hot loaves, dishes of boiled buttered leeks, and pots of jellied eels made their way from hand to hand. When the platter of thick slices of beef arrived, Edmund took two.

"Don't stuff yourself, Edmund," Hunred said.

Edmund growled his reply: "I'm saving some for Merewyn and mother!" and wrapped the slice of juicy meat in the flat soft loaf. With difficulty he squeezed it into his belt pouch.

Only then did Edmund dig into the food himself, realizing all at once how ravenous he was, and thirstily drank the weak but flavorful barley beer that stood in the pottery cup at his place.

Musicians played brightly on harp and pipes, and hall women brought round pitchers of beer to refill the cups. But soon Osbert stood up, and the reeve shouted for quiet. The thegn lifted up his beautifully worked silver cup and said, "Friends, thanks be to God, though some places suffer this year, Aelfsdene has a good harvest."

"So it is!" "Good Harvest!" People drank and cheered.

"But this is no ordinary harvest season. This very day, a holy company has come among us, bearing with them the greatest saint of Northumbria."

Awkward silence. These people wanted to have their harvest merriment, and probably to dance and likely to get drunk. And now their lord was talking religion!

"I have invited Bishop Eardwulf and his people to stay the winter," Osbert went on, looking around at faces suddenly sober. He paused just long enough before saying, "But he refused me. Those who bear the saint will not make themselves a burden to their hosts."

You could practically taste the relief in the hall, and Edmund observed with admiration how Osbert now won them over to his excitement about building a church. People began to ask, "How long will you stay, Bishop?" and "When can my children be baptized?" and "May we see the holy coffin?"

Bishop Eardwulf gave smiling and positive answers to all this, and promised a mass in the morning. "Now, soon I must go to sing nocturnes with my monks, and leave you to your harvest celebration. But first, we will have a story."

chapter fourteen

A MURMUR RIPPLED THROUGH THE HALL WHEN HE gestured at Aelfleda and she stood up, leaning on her walking stick. A woman, and such a young woman, to address the gathering?

But Osbert himself left the platform to take her by the hand, while a chair was set in front of the table for her.

The harper at the back of the hall played a few anticipatory notes as the crowd settled. Aelfleda sat, hands folded in her lap, gazing round the hall. She met each and every pair of eyes, until the silence was complete. The harper caught her eye again and plucked the strings decisively. Then she began, closing her eyes and putting her palms together as if in prayer. After a moment her eyes flashed open and she began to speak in a sing-song voice:

The man of God Cuthbert came to live
on the Island of Farne alone.
All alone with God he meant to stay—
just Cuthbert, God, and the birds of Farne.

Her arms and fingers moved to make pictures, almost, as she talked of Cuthbert and God and Farne and birds. Osbert sat at Aelfleda's feet, a childlike openness and admiration on his face while she told of the many birds of Farne who flocked about the holy man.

The listeners grew quieter as Aelfleda's arms and voice moved up and down, building in the air the tall stone wall around Saint Cuthbert's little hermitage, her cupped hands forming the boat that bobbed on the waves about the island, carrying the monks who came to visit him.

People laughed with delight as her voice suddenly mimicked a raven's cry to perfection. "The bold and greedy ravens!" she called them. The ravens stole straw from the roof of the saint's guest house and flew away cackling and defiant when he scolded them. And then next day returned . . . Again Aelfleda croaked like a raven, and to the astonishment of all, an answer came flying in through the open hall door, over the heads of many folk from the yard who had gathered at the threshold to listen.

Riddle took up a perch on a crossbeam before the storyteller. Edmund's breath caught for a moment as Aelfleda faltered at seeing her dead brother's pet. But then she croaked back at the bird, and Riddle again scolded her. As they fought with their voices, the audience's laughter rose to a roar like a gathering tide.

Then slowly Aelfleda got to her feet, leaning on her staff, and raised her arm to point at the raven, intoning in a deep voice the words of Saint Cuthbert: "In the name of Jesus Christ, I command you—stop taking what is not yours!"

The words seemed to hang there, and the listeners held their breath. Riddle's tirade gradually subsided, and then Edmund dared to whistle. Riddle preened a moment and then flew to

Edmund's shoulder. Edmund rewarded him with a bit of meat from his plate.

The hall folk laughed and clapped, and Aelfleda sat down in the chair once more, smiling in satisfaction.

"Next day the raven came back, bearing a lump of lard..."

Edmund, suddenly inspired, stood up, the bird in one hand and a chunk of beef fat he had carved off the meat on the other. With his thumb atop Riddle's toes, he gently moved his fist up and down, causing the bird to open his wings as if flying as he carried it over to Aelfleda. Turning toward the audience he held up the bird in one hand and the fat in the other.

Aelfleda never missed a beat at his unplanned dramatization of her tale.

"The bird bowed down in penitence and gave the saint his gift..." and then suddenly she rose again, beckoning to Osbert. His eyes widened and he mouthed, "Me?" pointing at himself.

Aelfleda patted the seat of the chair, and when Osbert sat himself there, she spoke on to the hall folk: "The next time his friends came to visit, Cuthbert used the lard to proof their shoes against the salt waves."

Edmund transferred Riddle to her hand, and playing the part of Saint Cuthbert he knelt at Osbert's feet, pretending to buff his shoes with the fat.

Aelfleda now looked all around the hall before speaking the saint's final word: "If only men would repent like the ravens, with prayers and bows and gifts!"

Applause and cheers burst forth. Osbert took Aelfleda, flushed and beaming, to her seat again, where he slid onto the bench beside her.

"I never saw such wonderful storytelling!" Osbert said to Aelfleda.

The reeve's daughter blushed. "Saint Cuthbert must have made Riddle help us out—he would not have done it on his own!"

They laughed, and Edmund laughed with them. But Hunred, eyes hard, got up abruptly and said in stiff disapproving tones, "Thank you for your hospitality, Lord Osbert. I shall be joining the monks now before the dancing and rowdiness begin."

OSBERT AND AELFLEDA REGARDED HUNRED WITH SURPRISE. Edmund was both astonished and appalled. The annoying thing about Hunred was how he greeted every event with eyes lifted to heaven, impassive as an oak tree. But speaking almost rudely to a lord who was hosting the holy company?

Hunred gave a quick nod of his head before ... well, *scuttling* away and out the door, like a crab running from a child chasing it at low tide.

They were spared any further awkwardness just then by the hall-thegns taking up the trestles and benches to clear the floor for the tumblers. Edmund felt only a mild interest in the entertainment to come, and decided instead to go outside and find Merewyn and his mother to give them the food he had saved.

Out in the yard, now under the stars and lit by several cook-fires, he spotted his sister and mother with Caris and some of the other Lindesfarne women. His mother's face was pinched with disapproval, and Merewyn's was shy and bewildered at the raucous scene. Some of the men already staggered about drunk, a fistfight had broken out amongst some young boys, and one young woman's veil had been snatched off by a laughing young man.

Caris seemed to care about none of it, her face pale and drawn, eyes unfocused.

"It's Edmund!" Merewyn cried with relief, tugging on their mother's arm, who brightened too when she saw him approach.

"Edmund, thanks be to God! We need a man to see us safely back to the camp!"

"Look, Edmund," said Merewyn. "I knew the moon rises late tonight, so I brought the lantern with a candle!"

"You," he said, "are the cleverest sister a man could have!" He enjoyed watching her pleasure in response, and traded her the pouch with the meat for the lantern. "I'll be back the moment I get it lit," he promised, and headed back across the yard toward the nearest cookfire.

In the pile of wood near the fire, he rummaged for a long-ish dry stick and thrust one end of it into the now dying flames. Waiting for it to catch, he looked up and saw Hunred standing on the other side of the fire, staring steadfastly at the open doors of the hall.

"What are you still doing here?" Edmund blurted.

Hunred turned his head in surprise; clearly he hadn't noticed Edmund's arrival. And then he returned to his intent watch upon the hall. "I'm waiting to speak to Stitheard."

Edmund frowned. "Well, why did you leave the hall then?"

The sharpness of Hunred's quick glance startled Edmund. "Didn't you see—can't you tell Osbert's after Aelfleda?"

Edmund's stick-end flared suddenly, and he scrambled to light the candle and shut the protective door of the lantern. "You're an idiot! Her father's right there, how could Osbert harm her even if he wanted to?"

"But he's wooing her! And Stitheard and the bishop too—he knows he can't have her without their approval!"

Edmund gaped. And then laughed. "I don't believe it—you're *jealous!*"

Hunred rounded on him, fury in his pale eyes. "Osbert wants to take her from the company—think of that! The best story-teller on Lindesfarne, our reeve's daughter, a true devotee of God and Saint Cuthbert! Osbert would take her from us, just because he can—because he can make her lady of this estate and give her gold and clothing and everything, anything she wants!"

Edmund stood dumbstruck. It was the longest, most impassioned speech he could ever remember hearing from Hunred. Hunred stood clenching and unclenching his fists. Suddenly he declared, "All right, I *will* go see Stitheard now—before Osbert can get his catch landed!"

Off he stamped, and Edmund, hearing his mother call, hurried back with the lit lantern.

"Could not Hunred join us?" she asked him in an aggrieved tone.

"He—he had to run an errand," said Edmund, still dazed at the peculiar exchange with his brother, the would-be monk.

Caris and a few other Lindesfarne women came along as Edmund led the escape from the rowdy yard, along the road and across the pasture to the camp, where some older folk had stayed to rest rather than join the festivities. His mother shared out to them some boiled eggs smuggled from the feast.

"I tell you, Edmund, the Aelfsdene women were not very welcoming!" she said.

"Indeed not," said Merewyn. "The meat at the fires was given to all at Lord Osbert's word—but did those women let us go first, as is right with guests?"

"Well," said Edmund. "The bishop said we would not stop

here long, but Osbert will see us hosted a while more at each of his other estates. That should take us to winter, at least."

"And then what? It's winter that matters!" said his mother.

"That it is," agreed one of the old fishwives. "My aching old bones need a rest. That snow in the hills nearly did me in!"

"The Saint will look after us," said Edmund, though he did not feel as certain as he hoped he sounded.

EDMUND AND THE OTHER BEARERS ATTENDED THE DAILY round of prayer with the monks. Hunred grew less talkative than ever, and Edmund grew more bored. But when Osbert asked a monk to stand by him at the services and translate the Latin for him, Edmund's messenger habits perked up suddenly, and he began to memorize phrase after phrase as the monk repeated the prayers in the common tongue.

The day of moving on came. As they set out at first light, autumn frost silvered the fields and leaves. It was to be a day of preaching and baptizing at Osbert's second estate only a few miles to the south, Crossensette, named for a high stone cross that stood on the land.

"Cuthbert himself once preached there, and Saint Aidan before him," the bishop said to Osbert, who walked alongside him as a pilgrim, leading his black horse by the bridle.

"I've always been told that Saint Oswald had the cross set up to proclaim his victory at the battle of Heavenfield, to show that Northumbria was a Christian kingdom."

"Should not both be true?" said Abbot Eadred, in one of his rare remarks. "Saintly kings and saintly bishops, both serving Christ and His Holy Gospel. Is this not what God wills?"

The bearers came to the weathered stone cross at mid-morning, and while the rest commenced to set up the tent, Edmund took the ox, Riddle riding its back, to drink at the little burn not far away. As he stood waiting for the animal to drink its fill, Edmund heard his name called and found Osbert approaching with his horse.

"Waes hal," Edmund said, nodding, as Osbert let his mount drink from the burn alongside the ox.

"Waes hal," he replied. "Edmund, I want to beg a favor of you."

"Me?" said Edmund. "I mean—I'll be glad to, but what can someone like me do for a thegn?"

"It's Caris," he said. "You were close as a brother to the man she was to have married."

Edmund nodded sadly. "She still refuses to stay?"

"This is the estate I would give her." Osbert opened his hand and gestured in a wide sweep. "But she won't even speak to me. There is something else . . . she may not accept from me. But if you would take it, and hold it till the company are far away—till she needs it . . ."

"I will, then, by God and by Saint Cuthbert," Edmund promised.

Osbert smiled. "Thank you!" He took a small leather bag from around his neck, opened it, and took out a linen-wrapped object. Gently he unfolded the cloth, and Edmund gasped at the glint of gold and gems. It was a pin, exquisitely worked knots of the bright metal with white and blue enamel filling the spaces between. It formed a cross in a circle.

Osbert wrapped it up again. "I found it in a box of my father's things after he died. It is a woman's style, but I never saw my mother wear it. And it is not of Northumbrian make—it is the work of Wealisc jewelsmiths. Caris's mother must have been wearing it when she was captured by my father in a raid against her people. So I count it as Caris's by right. You must tell her this when the time comes to give it to her." He put the pin back in the pouch and placed the leather thong over Edmund's head, and Edmund tucked it inside his tunic.

Osbert gave the ox a pat on the neck. "I wish I were coming with you." His eyes were alight in a strange way that reminded Edmund of Hunred, of all people. "Oh, Edmund, if I did not have responsibilities ... and ... well ..."

"It's Aelfleda, isn't it?"

Osbert's face flushed. "I asked the bishop. I asked her father. But oh, my friend—I'm afraid to ask her!"

For once Edmund did not know what to say. How could he encourage Osbert to take Aelfleda from the company? And yet— Osbert was a good man, and Aelfleda would own lands ...

Osbert looked shamefaced. "I'm sorry—I should not speak of this to you, when your brother hopes to win her too."

"Hunred? No, he wants to be a monk!"

Osbert gave him an odd look, then after a moment said, "It may be he doesn't know just what he wants." He sighed, and took his horse by the bridle again. "It doesn't matter, does it—in the end, it's only what Aelfleda wants. So here I am, Edmund— thegn and warrior and lord of estates, and all I care about is two women, and there's not a thing I can do to make either of them stay if they choose not."

"I'm sorry," said Edmund, and then they each took their animal and left the waterside.

chapter fifteen

IN THE TWELVEMONTH THAT FOLLOWED, THE COMPANY stayed at one estate after another as they made their way down the Rede Valley to the old wall where the Romans had once guarded against the barbarians on the borders of their vast ancient empire. Many of the stones had been taken away for building since those days, but still the spine of the wall stretched all along the River Tyne, west to Luel and east to Tynemouth and the sea. There were too many Danes about Tynemouth in the east, and Abbot Eadred's monastery of Luel in the west, they heard, was in ruins. So late in autumn, the increasing reluctance of their fellow Northumbrians to host them finally turned the company south and west, toward the bleak moors, along a hard frosty road south of the river.

One morning Abbot Eadred, who had come to walk alongside the cart with them, was talking about his old home monastery at Luel. Stitheard was leading the ox, and Hunred and Edmund walked on either side of the cart forward of the axle.

"I am only glad the brothers have all escaped," said Eadred, "some to Hwitern, some to Ireland."

"Ireland!" said Hunred, in a rare outburst. "The land of the saints! Father Abbot, could we not take the holy Cuthbert to one of the monasteries there, away from the invaders?" Edmund looked across the ox's back at Hunred's enraptured countenance and rolled his eyes. But when silence followed from Eadred, Stitheard, and the bishop, a sudden dread rose up in him.

It took several more paces for the bishop to say, in a careful undertone, "We will seek God's will. But I charge you all—speak not a word of such things in the hearing of the company!"

And they went on. As the early evening began to draw in, Brother Aethelbert, now mounted on a horse given them by Osbert, came galloping up. "We must leave this road and turn further south across the moors. I spoke to a man at the ford across the next burn, and he says the estate is under a Dane. And the next two beyond it, though that is all he knows. He does not think the Danes will trouble to chase us, but the people will not welcome us. The harvest in most of Westmoringaland was poor this year, and already there is sickness."

Stitheard let out a groan, and the bishop turned and gave him a sharp look. "We will go on then," Eardwulf said firmly, "as we always do, with God and Cuthbert!"

So they camped in a desolate place on the moor that night, and Edmund had to stamp his feet to keep warm as he tramped in a wide watch circle about the monks while they prayed around the coffin. People huddled about their fires, and the only sounds Edmund heard from them in the night were the cries of one or two small children. When the monks ended their midnight chanting, the distant howl of a wolf rang across the bleak hills. Riddle hunched on Edmund's shoulder, bristling at the eerie cry. Edmund tensed at the sound, but it was the replies of several more wolfish voices that made his throat go dry. When Franco took over his guard duty, Edmund lay awake nearly till dawn, fearing to hear them again and closer, but he did not. Not this time.

In the morning, half the chickens had frozen to death.

THE WINTER WENT FROM BAD TO WORSE, AND MOVING southward didn't spare them the frost and snow. Sometimes they found hospitality, sometimes not; more than once, when they did, they had to leave behind some members who fell ill. Aelfleda's donkey lamed, so she traded it for more chickens for the company and went on with the rest, limping herself as she leaned on her staff. Edmund wondered if Osbert had ever actually asked her to marry him. And if he had . . . was she sorry she hadn't said yes?

One day on the moors, they came across a strange breed of sheep with curled horns and shaggy fleece. They had seen no shepherd's botl near, and Stitheard sent men out in several directions to look for people. The bishop sent his mounted messenger ahead to investigate too, but he met no man and found no settlement near. "No dogs, no shepherds, nothing," Brother Aethelbert reported. "These sheep herd themselves, it seems!"

"Then they're wild!" said Stitheard. "Thanks be to God!"

"Amen," said the bishop. Abbot Eadred looked troubled, but then, he never ate meat under any circumstances.

They called a halt for the night, and a party of laymen went out to catch sheep. They came back triumphant with four, Riddle circling above with great excitement. They butchered two, bestowing the fleeces on the two youngest infants in the company. Edmund was startled when it dawned on him that the company now included a half-dozen children who had never known Lindesfarne.

The men tethered the other two sheep to bring along with the company, though the sheep were none too cooperative.

A full belly made for a good night, despite the hard ground and freezing air. Even the howling of the wolves did not trouble Edmund much when he did his watch round. He heard them every night now, and had even seen them approach within a few rods of the large group at times; but the laymen of the company, who also kept a regular night watch, easily drove them off by pelting them with stones and brandishing fiery sticks.

The haliwerfolc straggled along the road in pale wintry sun next day, more cheerful than they had been for weeks. Edmund was walking at Lindo's head once more when Cuthwin ran panting up to the bishop from the front of the column. "My lord bishop! Danes! There are Danes!"

"Calm yourself!" the bishop said sternly. "How many, how close?"

"Two. On horses. And they are trotting up to see you with Brother Aethelbert in the middle, and they are angry! The sheep belong to someone named Jarl Einarr!"

Stitheard groaned, and Eadred crossed himself, muttering, "*Kyrie eleison!*"

It was not quite so bad as it had been with Thorstein's men at Gateham. One of the horsemen was this Jarl Einarr's reeve, and the sheep were *not* wild, he told them in mostly passable English, looking at them as if they were idiots. The sheep breed was brought from his homeland, and they were *haefted*—which, he explained, meant they had now been raised to know their territory on this *fell*, which was what the Danes called the moor. "And now you will release these sheep, and pay Jarl Einarr for the theft!"

Edmund had to look away as Bishop Eardwulf humbled himself before the invaders and begged their mercy. The two Danes wandered up and down the lines, looking for anything of value. They discovered the new sheepskins, which they tore away from the mothers and their babies, cursing in Danske.

The man who was not the reeve wanted to take *thralls*. He was looking at some of the women and older children, so Edmund knew the word meant "slaves." Suddenly his thoughts went to the pin Osbert had given him for Caris, which he had not yet handed over to her, not being sure of the right time. It lay snug inside his tunic in its little leather pouch.

But the reeve did not look impressed at the quality of the prospective slaves, nor most of their livestock and ragtag belongings. He looked suspiciously at the cart with the saint's coffin. And the processional cross borne by one of the monks—not the gilded one, which was now buried in a secret trove in the Cheviots somewhere, but a plain wooden one. *"Halig?"* he asked.

"Holy, yes," the bishop answered. "We bear the bones of a saint."

"My wife serves the White Christ," he said. "But not I!" He tapped at a token shaped like an upside-down hammer on a heavy silver chain resting on his leather vest. "Thor is a god for men, and Odin is wise!" His horse did a little dance, snorting, and Riddle suddenly called in a scolding voice from Edmund's shoulder. The reeve looked in surprise at the bird, and the other man gasped and said something in Danske tunga.

The reeve said to Edmund, "How come you by Odin's bird?"

"He is Saint Cuthbert's bird!" Edmund said, indignant.

"Steady," Stitheard said to him under his breath.

The reeve narrowed his eyes at Edmund and the raven, then held out his hand. "Give him to me."

Edmund couldn't speak for a moment, a lump forming in his throat. He shook his head, and though the Dane's brows lowered menacingly at him, he said, "I can't give him to you. He isn't mine. He does what he wants, goes where he wants."

"Fetch me one of those empty chicken cages," barked the man.

Edmund stood with his mouth open, as without warning Hunred grabbed Riddle with both hands, pinning his wings. The reeve's helper came back with the cage, and Hunred shoved Riddle through the door and secured it. Riddle cursed as only a raven can. And then the reeve made Brother Aethelbert get off the company's only horse and turn the reins over to him. "Not again!" Aethelbert muttered under his breath.

"An amusing bird and a half-starved horse—fah! This is little payment for the fine sheep you took, *Engel-monn*," he said to the bishop, "let alone the insult of stealing from my jarl. But for my wife's sake, I will let you go without harm." As he and the man with Riddle turned to ride off, he laughed at them. "If I were you, *Engel-folk*, I would stay on this road, and keep on going till you reach the sea!"

THEY TOOK THE REEVE'S CONTEMPTUOUS ADVICE BECAUSE they had no better plan. After long, desolate wandering, they came out of the hills to Angle-held lands, where the charity of Christmastide won the company a slight, grudging welcome at a place called Workington, by Derwentmouth on the west coast. When they first arrived, Edmund thrilled, even in the grim gray days of Advent, to the salt air and the sound of waves that he had missed so badly.

The place was mostly made up of half-Wealisc folk, conquered by Northumbrian kings long ago in Cuthbert's day. Now their church was burnt and monks killed, and they were impoverished but otherwise not harmed by the thieving, bullying Danes. "Whoever rules away in Eoforwic, now Halfdan's dead, pays little heed to us out here, for good or ill," the local thegn told them. He had a Wealisc look about him, a flattish face and dark hair, and the Wealisc sing-song way of speaking.

Then he grinned ruefully. "We are used to conquerors here. Just like when the lords were English—we send the barrels of fish they demand twice a year, and try to keep out of their attention!"

Just after the feast of Christ Mass, people began to fall ill. The thegn had insisted the bishop take a tiny guest hut, and the monks and bearers lodged in a barn with the saint's relics; but the rest lived still in their half-open tents, even those who were ill. One morning, the novice Franco and Brother Aidan woke sneezing and coughing, so Stitheard dispatched Edmund to the hall to fetch a hot draught of mint and *maegthen* for them. While the thegn's wife filled the cups he had brought, Edmund overheard an old man hacking and coughing at the fireside. As the healing draught warmed the clay cups Edmund held in grateful hands, the old man raised his voice: "Hell take all these strangers and their saint! They eat our food and bring sickness with them!"

Edmund went pale at the blasphemy and opened his mouth to bark a retort, but the thegn's wife said quickly, "Don't mind him. He's old and cranky. Here, take some cheese for your friends too," she said, and tucked a piece in the crook of his elbow while he held the cups.

So he thanked her and went out, aware that not just the old man but others in the hall were watching him go. After delivering the draughts and cheese to the patients, Edmund went like the messenger he still wished he was to report the old man's words. He found the bishop in the small guest hut.

Eardwulf's lips went thin and tight at the news. Then he said, "I think perhaps he meant you to overhear, Edmund. We will leave tomorrow."

chapter sixteen

Edmund was sent to fetch Stitheard, Abbot Eadred, and, mystifyingly, Hunred. In the tiny hut, they all stood crowded about the bishop, who sat upon his narrow cot.

To Hunred and Edmund he said, "I am sending you both with Stitheard down to the waterside. We must have a ship for Ireland, at once. For Cuthbert." Before they could reply, he went on, "All the bearers, that's seven, and Abbot Eadred and myself make nine passengers. As little else as we can manage. I count on you two, who are fishermen, to see that the ship is sound and the crew competent."

"But it's January!" Edmund said, aghast.

"The less likely any Danes will pursue us," the bishop said sharply. "And as you yourself heard today, Edmund, we are not wanted here—just as we are not wanted anywhere in Northumbria, it seems, even among English Christian folk!"

The bitterness hit Edmund like a rogue wave. For a moment the pain and discouragement mastered Eardwulf's features, and Edmund thought with a shock, *He's grown so old!*

Eadred smoothed the awkward moment. "My friends, is it not possible sea conditions on the passage to Ireland may be less harsh than in your North Sea off Lindesfarne?"

Not bloody likely, in January, Edmund thought and almost said. It was just as well that Hunred gave a more tempered, "They may . . ." But even he looked doubtful.

"But passage for only nine—what of the company!" cried Edmund.

Stitheard gripped his shoulder, restraining him. "The company is safer without us, boy," he said bleakly.

Edmund's neck grew hot. He looked directly at the bishop and said, "You really believe that?"

"Edmund! Watch your tongue!" Hunred snapped, but the bishop waved it away.

"Edmund," he said, and looked around at all of the small desperate group, "if we do not or cannot believe, still we can hope. We must. Eadred—the passage money?"

The abbot produced a small woolen bag that clinked as he set it in Stitheard's open palm. Stitheard's brow furrowed. "I thought the Danes took our last coin at Gateham . . . when did we come by this?"

Eadred let the bishop answer, which he did with a sigh. "Just now, Stitheard. We've sold Lindo and the cart to the thegn here at Workington."

Stitheard gasped. "That holy animal—to these half-Wealas? I raised him from a calf, trained him myself to plough and cart. He was *mine*! I gave him gladly to Saint Cuthbert—but not to be sold like an old goat to strange folk!"

Eardwulf's voice went hard. "Do you think I would do this if I had any other choice, Stitheard? The Workington thegn refused our other old ox and would only have Lindo."

The big man was breathing hard. Only when Derwin died had Edmund seen him so distraught.

Finally Stitheard forced words out again. "My son is lost, and no one is left to care for my lame daughter. For love of the saint and his haliwerfolc, she turned down the chance to be Osbert's lady in Aelfsdene. If there is any gratitude in you, bishop, then there will be something in that coin pouch for Aelfleda, to help her when we are gone to Ireland!"

After a pained silence, the bishop said in a milder tone, "Stitheard, I would have none of the company suffer, least of all Aelfleda. You and our fisher-bearers shall bargain with the ship owners. Whatever can be saved from the purse, let it be Aelfleda's."

Stitheard relaxed finally. "Thank you, my lord bishop. If my Aelfleda is seen to, then all is well." He kissed the bishop's hand, and when Edmund and Hunred had done likewise, the three set out for the riverside.

Once they were on the road, Edmund said, "But what will happen to the company, Stitheard? Where will they go?"

"Am I a prophet?" Stitheard roared.

Edmund pulled up short in the middle of the rutted, muddy road, stung by the rebuke. But he could not stop himself saying, "This can't be right! If Eadred had a dream, as he did about leaving Lindesfarne, why doesn't he say so? How can we take Cuthbert away from his land and his people?"

"Edmund, you took oath to obey when you were made a saintbearer," said Hunred, in his most irritatingly reasonable tone.

Edmund rounded angrily on him, fists clenched, but Stitheard grabbed him by the sleeve and cut in, "Hunred, let me see *you* obey too! Get on ahead and start looking for a ship!"

Edmund glared in smug triumph at Hunred's astonished look.

After a moment Hunred said, "Yes, Stitheard," and went off at a fast-paced stalk through the wintry drizzle.

When he was out of earshot, though, Stitheard smacked Edmund up the side of his head.

"Ow!" Edmund grabbed his stinging ear and stared at Stitheard in astonishment.

"Do I have your attention now, boy?"

Edmund said nothing, but did not look away from Stitheard's frowning face.

"I have known you and your brother both from your father's knee. And it was all fine for Hunred to give himself airs on Lindesfarne, and for you to sulk there too, like a cat whose dinner was stolen."

"Sulk!" said Edmund, indignant. "I do *not* sulk, I—"

"*Edmund!*" said Stitheard.

Edmund's mouth snapped closed, but he felt the angry words wriggling to get out, like fresh-caught fish that were not yet out of breath or out of fight.

Stitheard went on, "On Lindesfarne I pitied you both as boys for the loss of your father. But we are not on Lindesfarne any more, and you are not boys any more. You accepted a holy service. You *will* hold your tongue, do you hear? If you have to bite till it bleeds."

Edmund stared at the ground, at his worn, torn leather shoes with the thong that had broken and was too short to lace the right one up properly. He did not say, *I just know it's wrong!*

"Now, Edmund, when we've found a ship for Ireland, you and Hunred can go see your mother and sister one last time. But you must *not* tell them a word of the plan. The people must not hear a word of it till we are ready to go—tomorrow if we can."

That's horrible! Edmund thought, and knew his face showed

his thought. But with not a word passing Edmund's lips, Stitheard overlooked his expression.

"Do you promise, then?"

Edmund nodded curtly. "Yes. I promise."

So they continued on their way to the riverside. Hunred came running to meet them. "I've found a man who will do it for less than anyone else, whatever they ask!"

THE SCRAWNY, SCRAGGLE-BEARDED LITTLE SHIP OWNER called Rhys wore a green cloak and tunic of surprising quality, but his leather shoes were as worn as Edmund's. Edmund guessed the man was less a successful trader than he was a—currently—successful gambler. And his gamble on this passage to Ireland would be this: He would save them money by not hiring sailors, and have his passengers themselves crew the ship on the voyage. It made the hair stand up on Edmund's neck. He and Hunred knew boats, but not one this size, and not these waters.

"Well?" said Stitheard as Edmund completed his inspection of the ship itself. There was nothing in its construction to find fault with; the seams looked tight enough, and there was adequate room to secure the coffin and their few other items of baggage amidships.

Edmund frowned up at the mast and the furled sail. "Is the sail in good repair? And the spare?"

"Good enough," said the ship owner, scratching his chin.

Edmund eyed the man suspiciously, but after all, it was Rhys's own skin as well if anything on his vessel failed.

"Well—it should do," he said reluctantly to Stitheard.

"Let us call it a bargain, then!" said Stitheard. "Off you

go, Edmund—run the word up to the bishop while we settle the details, and then the day is yours. Have supper with your family."

"Thank you, Stitheard!" Edmund said gratefully. How long the voyage would be he wasn't sure, but any amount of time stuck in a boat with Hunred was not something he looked forward to. A run was just what Edmund needed.

chapter seventeen

MEREWYN'S BEAMING FACE LIGHTENED THINGS, AS it always did, when she greeted Edmund, and his mother too perked up at his arrival. The sun itself worked a bright little hole through the clouds, which looked as if they were thinking of moving off toward the hills.

"It isn't even a feast day, how is it you come to us now?" Merewyn bubbled.

"Oh—you know—there's nothing much for us to do at the hall," he said vaguely, gazing about the camp because he knew his eyes would betray him. He jumped up then, saying, "Oh, look, there's Caris, I have to take her a message," and ran off.

Caris was on her way out of the camp, taking two buckets toward the burn. Edmund jogged quickly alongside and said, "I'll carry those for you."

She greeted him with a surprised smile. "Waes hal, Edmund!" Handing over the buckets, she asked, "What brings you here?"

"Stitheard gave me leave to come visit."

"Are we going to be moving on again soon?"

"Ah—" he hesitated.

"What's wrong with you?" she said, peering closely at him.

"Nothing!" Caris could always spot things quicker than most people.

"Nothing? Well, what kind of nothing, then?"

Edmund glanced back at the camp. No one else was headed this way, but he felt he wanted to be further out of their hearing. "Let's get down to the water first."

"All right," she said, and began tripping along smartly enough that Edmund hardly had to shorten his own longer stride to match pace with her.

The burn gurgled, icy cold and a little muddy. "I suppose that's a sign of spring coming, at least," he said as he dipped the first bucket in.

"Edmund, stop making silly conversation. What is it you aren't saying?"

She stood on the bank with arms folded. Edmund set the full bucket down at her feet, snickering at her impatient expression and shaking his head.

Caris's mouth fell open and she set her hands on her hips. "And now you're laughing at me! I'll take my buckets, thank you!"

She made a lunge for the handle of the full bucket, but as her fingers closed around the thick-woven hemp, Edmund latched onto her wrist. She tugged away, the bucket rocked, and water splashed over her shoes and already bedraggled hem.

"You pea-brain!"

"I'm sorry, I'm sorry!"

She shoved the half-emptied bucket back at him with a sigh of exasperation, then retreated up the bank to a somewhat less muddy spot under a winter-bare willow tree to empty her shoes and wring out her stockings.

"I'm sorry," he said again, when he had filled both buckets and set them on a level spot.

Caris pursed her lips. "Do get on with it, Edmund."

Edmund took the pouch from his neck with a sigh and handed it to her. Frowning, she opened it.

"What's this?" She stared at the pin lying on the open linen wrapping in her palm, then glanced quickly up at Edmund. "Where did you get it?"

"From Osbert. He said it's Wealisc work, and it was your mother's."

Caris's free hand clapped over her mouth as she stared at the intricately patterned gold. Then her head came proudly up. "So, now do you believe me, Edmund son of Tida?"

"What?"

"Derwin said you would never believe I was a king's daughter!"

Edmund shrugged. "Caris, Osbert said your mother was just some Wealisc thegn's daughter, taken in a raid in his father's young days. Think about it—if she'd had royal rank, the Wealas would have bought her back. What's more important is, Osbert says you're his sister."

Her cheeks colored as she looked away. "Half-sister. Not . . . a proper, rightly-born sister. And his mother hated me!"

"That isn't his fault! She's long dead. Why didn't you take Osbert's offer—he would have found you a husband who wouldn't care that your mother was a slave!"

O God and Cuthbert, save me! thought Edmund, *now she's crying. What do I do with a girl who's crying?* "Caris?" Panic rose in his throat. One hand stole toward her, but he took it back, afraid of upsetting something again the way he had upset the bucket. *O God, please make her stop! Why* is *she crying?*

As usually happened when Edmund had too many thoughts, they started spilling out his mouth. "Caris? *Why* are you crying?"

She gave him an astonished look, and the weeping turned to a wail.

"Caris, please stop!" he glanced nervously across the meadow. "People are going to hear!"

The weeping got quieter. A little. Clutching the pin in one hand and wiping her face on her veil with the other, Caris subsided into slight, shuddering sobs.

"I couldn't ever be a lady, not really," she said in a small voice. The tears still glimmered on her lashes when her eyes met Edmund's.

After a moment Edmund said, "Well—you won't be, so that's all right, isn't it?" And then he kissed her.

That's what you do, he thought with surprise. *The girl is crying, her eyes are like jewels, and you kiss her.*

And then he sprang away. She gasped aloud. Their eyes were still locked.

"I'm sorry!" he shouted, backing away. "I only came to bring you the pin! I'm sorry, I have to go—we're going, we're taking Cuthbert to Ireland, loading him on a ship tonight and leaving on the morning tide. Just the bearers and the bishop and abbot, no one else—please, please, Caris, don't tell anyone or Stitheard will flay me!"

"What? Leaving? Edmund!"

"I'm sorry!" He turned and ran. Not like a messenger on an urgent errand—more like a coward deserting a field of battle. He headed west across the meadow, avoiding the camp, and on toward the south coastal road. He ran until his sides began to ache. It happened much sooner than he expected, and he was bewildered to find himself so out of training. Bent double and gasping, he again fell under the assault of his thoughts. *I can't do that. I can't kiss girls, I'm a saint-bearer.*

But I just did.

And: *And she didn't even slap me. Caris—I kissed Caris, and she didn't slap me!*

Edmund growled at his own inner voice and straightened again, breathing in through his nose, out through his mouth. He flexed his ankles a little, set his face for the distant curve of the muddy road, breathed deep and began to run again, this time at a more deliberate lope. It was not a race; there was no one chasing him but his own thoughts, and no runner on earth could outpace those. *Derwin would hold me in check,* he thought, and imagined his friend still running at his side, the way he used to do on Lindesfarne. This road ran along the coast, and it was almost like home—beneath the sound of his feet pounding on the road, from the right he could hear a distant *shush* of waves. Gulls mewed above, a sound to break the heart, and Edmund tasted the tang of salt on his lips.

A stone cross loomed on the hill ahead. As Edmund drew nearer, he saw that it marked a crossroads. His road continued south, while the cross road emerged from a woodland and led up to the cross and then down to the western shore on his right.

As he drew nearer, he saw that half of one arm of the cross was broken off, and on the face nearest Edmund, great black marks marred the surface of the shaft. Edmund slowed to a walk and scanned all directions, a messenger once more on the lookout for signs of trouble.

But not a soul appeared in any direction. Edmund began to feel the chill of the January sea breeze as it buffeted his ears on the hilltop. A closer look at the cross, and Edmund read the riddle thus: the break showed some weathering, and the marks, made with charcoal, were beginning to fade—likely made in the last few years. And certainly the Danes had made them, for he could still discern the shape of the upside-down hammer that proclaimed the power of their god Thor. Danes had been here, probably the same year they burned the little church at Workington. Though no one was in sight now, they might have settled in the next place south, and the next, and the next . . .

The wind gusted, and out on the water whitecaps began to appear. Gazing at the mutilated cross, Edmund felt a gloom creeping into his heart. This was why the bishop and abbot had decided to flee to Ireland.

The heathen Danes are here to stay. Lindesfarne is a dream, I'll never see it again.

Edmund wanted to weep, but couldn't. Too many feelings had already washed over him today, leaving him numb, like a sailor near-frozen and half-dead in his boat in the storm. Edmund rested his head against the shaft of the cross. *How could I have kissed Caris? My friend is dead, and I took his pet raven—lost it, too!—and now I'm kissing his betrothed!*

No. He *wasn't* kissing her, not again. He was going away to Ireland with Saint Cuthbert. *Even though I think it's wrong!* No devastation and conquest could make it right to take Cuthbert away from his haliwerfolc, away from his land of Northumbria. But Edmund was only the very most junior of the saint-bearers. He had no right to speak his mind to the bishop and abbot, who had surely made their plan in great agony of heart.

He kissed the shaft of the crippled cross, then made its sign upon his own forehead. "*Kyrie eleison,*" he whispered, and headed north again.

By the time he approached the Workington lands, cold rain was pelting down, turning the road treacherous beneath his feet. Edmund had to give up and walk. Caris stood in the middle of the road waiting for him, arms folded. He slowed to a stop less than a rod away from her, swallowing hard.

The rain streamed down both their faces. After a moment's standing and staring, Caris dropped her arms to her sides, paced up to him and stopped within arm's length. Then she smacked his face. "That," she said, "is for kissing me. And that," she said, hitting his other cheek with her other hand, "is for running away!"

Then she turned and stalked back to the camp in the pasture, leaving him with burning cheeks.

The rain turned to sleet.

The wagon wheels creaked along the road to the boat launch. It was still fully dark, and lanterns swung from the hands of many of the monks who accompanied the bearers in desolate silence. The freezing rain had passed on, replaced by drier air from the northeast, and the wintry breath of the walkers smoked in the yellow light. To Edmund the groan of the wheels, repeated with each slow revolution, sounded like a warning voice: *wrong . . . wrong . . . wrong.*

The shipmaster awaited them at the landing place on the bank of the Derwent. The bearers paused and unloaded the holy coffin with great care while the monks gathered around in silence, lest they wake any of the Derwentmouth folk. Both the coffin and the great Gospel book were now packed within outer crating, with packing materials to protect them from the wet.

"How soon do we leave shore?" the bishop asked the shipmaster, while Hunred and Edmund secured the coffin amidships.

"Patience," said the little man. "The tide doesn't run out again till about tierce. At first light we'll launch and row out into midriver. Then the current will help us along to the sea in time to catch the tide."

Edmund checked and rechecked every rope on the coffin, on the little vessel, and all their other meager baggage. He kept at it partly not to look at Stitheard, who was reluctantly turning Lindo the ox over to one of the monks for return to the new owner at Workington hall. Edmund's stomach clenched to see the big man's shoulders so bowed, and to hear the catch in his voice as he spoke soothingly to the ox.

The bishop, standing on the shore, called all his monks to kneel before him. But the moment he had blessed them, his voice rose sharply: "Stitheard! Come launch the ship—now!"

Edmund looked up in alarm from tightening the knots that bound the Gospel book to the coffin and saw the bishop marching down the bank to the boat. Up atop the riverbank, the black of the sky was fading to gray, but it was the lanterns and torches raised there that made Edmund's heart leap suddenly—half with hope, half with fear. The layfolk of the company, led by Cuthwin's father the smith, had gathered there with grim faces. But it was Edmund's own mother who gave voice to their outrage and grief.

"I didn't want to believe it—you are going without us! God curse you!"

The smith cried out too. "What kind of bishop takes the people's saint from them?"

The chorus was as loud as it was unruly: "Where do we go now?" "Who will take care of us?" "How can our people ever defeat the invader without our Cuthbert?"

Stitheard, still among the monks, raised his hands, ready to respond, but the bishop, now alongside the ship, barked his name again. The shipmaster cursed as he and Edmund and the others hopped out, took hold of the sides, and began heaving the little craft forward into the water.

The reeve turned to look at Eardwulf. A tug-of-war passed over his face, and Edmund thought for a moment he might turn on the bishop and go back with his ox to his daughter and his friends. But then he took a deep shuddering breath, and stumped toward the ship and out into the water.

Edmund's mother was wailing now, and his and Hunred's names were in her cries. At her side Edmund finally saw Caris. When their eyes met, she looked guiltily away, but then raised her head again in proud defiance. She was glad she had told everyone, and Edmund found he was glad too. He smiled, and she smiled back.

Stitheard joined the others; the ship was fully in the water now, and they all clambered aboard. The monks still stood between the bearers and the layfolk. Attempts at reason shattered like ocean spray on the rock of their outrage. People cried out now against Stitheard for a traitor, and all the bearers heard their names too, as some pleaded and others berated them. Hunred hid his face, hunching low in the boat, as his and Edmund's mother kept up her hail of pleas. But Edmund saw the stark despair in her face, as he had not seen it since that day long ago when he came home from the sea without his father.

"Come back to your sister!" she cried, pulling Merewyn forward.

Merewyn added her voice and the entreaty of brimming eyes. "Edmund!"

"I'm sorry!" he shouted.

"Out oars!" cried Rhys, and each of them found a bench and an oar, struggling to get the blades into the water and strokes at the same rhythm.

Scuffling broke out on shore, as the layfolk pushed at the monks who stood in the way. One of the monks lost his footing and slid down the bank, the wall of monks broke apart, and the layfolk surged forward to the river's edge and even into the water itself.

"Stroke! Stroke!" bellowed the shipmaster, and the little ship he called *The Cunning Fox* labored away from the mob.

"*Hunred!*" Aelfleda's scream broke above the din. "You promised me! You can't go! You can't!"

Edmund stared at her in horror. His eyes met Caris's again. She stood with lips pressed together, angry tears gleaming in her eyes. Edmund felt like his heart was being torn to pieces. Why didn't the bishop just change his mind?

The chorus of misery from the shore swelled louder and shriller than ever, and the bearers dug their oars into the water with desperate abandon. A wave of names and curses and wordless cries broke over the retreating boat. The water seemed thick as honey as they strove to pull away from the landing place, and the shipmaster cursed them in languages Edmund had never heard before.

A dimly smoldering sun peeked over the treed hills to the east as the little ship slowly struggled toward midriver. Still the shouts and wailing could be heard from the shore. Edmund felt the current under the wooden bottom of the ship, and the rowers finally fell into a slow, steady rhythm, letting the river do most of the work. After the shipmaster called, "Up oars, you land-rats!" Edmund sat listening, straining for a last sound from the shorebound company; but the rush of the wind overwhelmed whatever still remained.

chapter eighteen

HEY RAISED THE SAIL AND WENT OUT FROM THE estuary on the tide into a calm sea in a light drizzle, with a following wind and red morning behind them. Before long, the perfectly mild rolling of the ship sent the landsmen all to the sides to empty their stomachs into the deep, but Edmund, Hunred, and Rhys the shipmaster kept to their posts. Edmund sat by the prow, scanning the horizon and feeling the chill salt air on his face. His heart should have swelled like the filling sail itself with pleasure at being back on the water after so long; but every knot they gained took them more speedily away from the haliwerfolc.

Abbot Eadred began the morning office, a little weakly. The feeble responses from the others did not discourage him. Before the service ended, though, Edmund could see white on the gray-green water. "Rough seas ahead!" he called. The *Cunning Fox* drew out from the shadow of a headland to the south, and as Edmund had feared, a choppy sea met them, buffeting them back like a large army repelling a cocky little invader.

The sail suddenly sagged, then billowed again the other way as the wind veered away to the southwest. The shipmaster cursed loudly as he wrestled with the tiller in the steersman's seat in the stern, trying to keep the course true. The vague pale gray overcast of the sky swiftly built in the west into a bank of belligerent-looking clouds, black as iron and with great heaped forms like clenched fists.

"Is this usual in these seas for January?" Edmund shouted back to the shipmaster, but what he really meant was, *How bad will it get?*

"Aye, it's naught, you expect a little roughness in the winter, don't you?" the man called back, but Edmund thought he looked less than confident now.

The swells grew deeper. Some of the bearers retched at the side again. Then the clouds bore down upon them, attacking them with icy arrows of sleet. Stitheard gave a low moan, and Edmund hated to see the strong man so badly out of his element, drained by the seasickness and beaten by the weather.

The troughs of water deepened, and the landsmen gasped in fear. Edmund was not afraid, not yet. And then a towering wave broke over the boat, taking the breath out of them all.

Edmund clung to the prow as the *Fox* heaved up again.

"Saint Cuthbert, save us!" cried Franco, clutching at the ropes that held the coffin in place amidships. The bishop intoned a low prayer, but the abbot was silent. And Hunred, to Edmund's disgust, was kneeling with arms up to heaven, eyes closed and lips moving.

"Hunred! Bail, you idiot!" Edmund screamed above the wind, scooping water with the bailing bucket stowed near his feet. The shipmaster, still braced against the tiller, added worse names as he ordered the others to help; there was another bucket elsewhere in the boat, but none of the others knew where to find it till Hunred sought it out. The rest used their hands.

The *Cunning Fox* bobbed helplessly on the waves. The shipmaster called on the bishop, who sat nearest him, to help him hold the tiller. And then the men cried out as a second giant wave reared up and slammed itself down on them.

Edmund gasped and coughed, bruised from head to toe. He was chilled to the bone, too, but he began bailing again at once, screaming at the others to keep it up too. The water in the boat was already higher than before.

Half the crew were lying flat out in the bottom of the boat, stunned by the power and intense cold of the water. The boat lurched again, and the rope that lashed the Gospel book to the coffin suddenly snapped. The book in its wrappings slid off into the pool of water sloshing about their feet.

"The book!" Edmund cried. He dropped the bailing bucket and made a lunge, sweeping the precious treasure up in his arms.

A third wave, roaring like the end of the world, slammed down atop them all. Edmund went down, clutching the Holy Book, and smacked his cheek against the rowing bench. When the wave subsided, the cries of the men broke out again, one rising above the rest in pain and panic.

"My arm!" yelled the shipmaster.

Edmund struggled to his knees in the water that now filled the boat nearly to the middle, and saw Rhys sprawled in the stern while the bishop wrestled hopelessly with the tiller. Franco was down with a cut on his temple, and most of the others lay stunned. Hunred was still clutching at the coffin.

"Take the book!" Edmund said, and shoved it at Hunred, who took it with one hand while holding on to one of the coffin ropes with the other. Edmund clambered atop the coffin itself and made his way over the stricken men to the stern. "Give me the tiller!" Edmund ordered the bishop, who yielded him the steersman's place gladly. "Anyone that's alive, get up and get bailing!" Edmund took the tiller and wrestled with it, while the others struggled to respond to his direction.

Something bumped them from below, and at the same moment Hunred cried, "Blood! The water is bloody!"

Edmund shouted, "Hunred, just keep hold of the—" but then the ship turned on its side. The half-dead men clung to whatever they could reach, crying out desperate prayers, and Edmund watched with horror as the Gospel book sailed from Hunred's grasp and splashed into the red-swirling sea.

"The Holy Book!" cried Abbot Eadred. "*Miserere nobis!* Cuthbert, pray for us!"

The shipmaster lost his grip on the rowing bench and hung half out the side. The bishop grabbed hold of the man's legs, and Edmund let go of the tiller to grasp the bishop's arm, anchoring them all with his own feet hooked under the steersman's bench.

The ship righted itself again. Edmund and the bishop dragged the shipmaster back to safety. The others sat or lay in the vessel, most of them stunned by the loss of the book as much as by the battering the sea had given them.

"O Cuthbert, who by your prayers confounded the heathen mockers and saved the monks who sailed at Wearmouth, pray God to save us now!" cried Abbot Eadred. "O God, forgive us our folly and bring us safe home again!"

Edmund did not know if the thought that came to him was from God and good or if it was his own and blasphemy, but he obeyed it at once as a crewman obeys the shipmaster's command. The thought was: *I will sail this ship true and be the answer to this prayer!*

Before he had even made a move, the sea began to settle, and the clouds opened in a steady drizzle. Beyond the clouds in the west he could see blue on the horizon. Edmund took the tiller and with fierce satisfaction put the *Fox* around to let her sail take the strong and steady wind that was blowing from the west. Soon the cloud and light rain passed on before them to the east, and the wind was blowing cold but friendly behind them. The bishop went forward to take Edmund's former post at the prow, and Edmund settled in the steersman's seat, holding the tiller easily now while Eadred fashioned a sling for Rhys's arm and the others finished bailing.

The last curtain of rain drew up from before them and moved eastward into the hills. The bishop, keeping lookout in the prow, exclaimed, "*Gloria Dei!*" and turned to the others with a glowing smile on his face. "The people must have left Derwentmouth and followed the shore to watch us all this while! They are standing on the beach south of the river waiting to welcome us back."

Before long they made landfall.

"Help us!" cried Edmund to the folk on shore as he leapt out into the icy surf up to his knees. The other bearers too plunged into the water and hauled on the boat's sides. Some of the laymen joined them, and soon the ship was drawn well up onto the beach, out of reach of the waves.

Edmund's mother fell on his neck, weeping and beaming. "God has brought you back to us!" she gushed, and then turned and did the same to Hunred. Edmund thought Hunred looked like death. His hollow eyes alarmed their mother too. "Here, now, I will have that wet cloak and you take mine!"

Women were crying and praising God and Saint Cuthbert,

and the monks in shamefaced but relieved silence helped gather driftwood for a fire. Edmund knew where the shipmaster's watertight tinderbox was stowed, and he fetched it out. The moment he turned it over to Cuthwin's father the smith, he found himself accosted by a tight-lipped Caris, who undid his sopping cloak, flung her own over his shoulders and fastened it tight. His energy spent, he fell to shuddering violently as he tried to clutch the woolen garment around him.

Friends and family shared cloaks with all the seafarers. The storm had passed so quickly over the beach and away into the hills to the east, it had rained only briefly on the haliwerfolc, and the driftwood was nearly dry. Helpful folk crowded about the storm survivors, forming a wall against the wind about the fire as it caught. The leech-monk had a look at the shipmaster's hurt arm and shook his head, clucking. No one else of the crew had anything but scrapes and bruises—those and utter exhaustion.

They were not yet fully dry when the bishop made his way out through protective ranks about the fire. The circle broke up, and he threw himself full-length on the pebbled shore before the monks, laymen, women and children, farmers, fishers, and hall folk of Lindesfarne, the far-traveled haliwerfolc of Saint Cuthbert.

"People of Cuthbert, forgive me! May God forgive me!"

Eadred likewise cast himself down in humility, tears streaming down his face. Edmund and the other bearers all fell to their knees, making the sign of the cross.

At last the smith had to get up and take the bishop by the arm. "Please, get up and help us, father in God. We forgive you. Come back to the camp and tell us what to do now!"

When they came back to Workington that afternoon, they did not take Cuthbert back to the barn, and the monks also vacated it to join the layfolk in their pasture camp. Cuthbert's coffin was laid on the baggage cart, and the monks gathered round to pray. The bishop declared the bearers free to rest from their ordeal. Despite his weariness, Edmund did not think he could sleep while the sun was still on its way down. He wanted to run again, but his worn and battered body would not obey, so he had to content himself with an aimless wander about the perimeter of the camp pasture. He found himself by some winter-blackened bramble bushes at the roadside, and to his dismay, as he rounded their edge he ran nearly into Stitheard and Hunred.

"And so you said *what* to her?" Stitheard demanded, his back to Edmund, whose jaw dropped. The air was charged as if with a close-approaching storm. Stitheard, brows down, had his fists raised to Hunred.

"Answer me, boy!" he barked, though Hunred was hardly a boy any more, his thin beard more reddish than the pale wheat-like hair that he still kept in an almost monk-like short crop. Hunred didn't even flinch, as if he were so defeated by life that he could barely stand anyway, and no new threat meant anything to him. Stitheard lunged for him, and Edmund grabbed at the reeve's massive and muscular arm in alarm.

"Stitheard, don't! We're the saint-bearers! We can't use violence—and on one another, what are you thinking!"

Stitheard shook him off, and Edmund went sprawling into the brambles. But the surprise distracted Stitheard. "Edmund? God curse it, boy, what are you doing sneaking up like that?"

"I didn't mean to!" Edmund extracted himself from the brambles, not caring about the rips in his tunic or the scratches on his arms.

Stitheard blew out a frustrated breath. Still Hunred stood silent, but he swallowed hard.

"Never mind," said Stitheard to Edmund, "Stay and witness."

"I—" *would rather not,* thought Edmund, but clamped his mouth shut. Stitheard furious, Hunred like a walking dead man . . . "her" could only mean Aelfleda. So Edmund stood by, terrified that he might have to get between the two, but not knowing what else to do.

Hunred shook his head slowly, his voice barely more than a whisper. "I know I promised her. *After* we find a home for the saint, we agreed. She and I. However long it might take. But that was before . . ."

"*Look* at me, you coward!"

Hunred obeyed, but he seemed drained of all feeling, not caring about Stitheard's disapproval or even hatred.

"So, my daughter is weeping right now because today you told her that you were taking back your promise to wed her one day?"

Bleak-faced, Hunred took a breath and nodded. "I lost the Holy Gospel book. I need to do penance. Whenever we do finally find a resting-place for the saint, I will be a monk for the rest of my days."

Edmund stared, thinking, *If Stitheard doesn't hit him now, I will!*

Stitheard folded his arms, and his face and voice went cold. "Do you think Bishop Eardwulf will let you take that vow," Stitheard said, "when you will have to forswear an earlier one to do so?"

For the first time Hunred hesitated. "I asked him already. He said yes. Stitheard, it wasn't truly an oath—just an agreement

Aelfleda and I made at Aelfsdene, that *if* and *when* we found a new home for the holy relics—"

"Stitheard," Edmund whispered. "Don't hit him. He *wants* you to hit him."

Stitheard stood immobile a while longer and then said, "Edmund, I am going now. *Before I kill him.*" Then he tramped off across the pasture toward the camp in the dusk.

Edmund and Hunred stood looking at each other.

Edmund swallowed. "Aelfleda turned Osbert down for *you?*"

Hunred nodded.

"Did you ever even believe we would find a place for Cuthbert, and you would have to *keep* that promise to her?"

Hunred shook his head and shrugged helplessly. "I *meant* to keep it, of course I did! But what if God didn't will it?"

Edmund stared at him in disbelief. "God? God didn't lose the Gospel book—you did! Tell me the truth—did you do that on purpose? To have a big sin to do penance for and not have to marry Aelfleda after all?"

"No!" Hunred shook his head, but looked puzzled. Maybe he didn't even know for sure himself what he had meant to do.

Edmund cursed him with words he had heard at some of the places the company stopped at but had never used before in his life. "I used to blame you for not being there, the day the storm took Father from the boat. But now I know—you would have been no use even if you *had* been there. You're a coward. You're no kin of mine, Hunred."

He turned to go. Hunred said, "It's worse than that."

Edmund closed his eyes, clenching his fists.

"I knew we shouldn't go to Ireland," said Hunred. "The night before we left, I dreamed the storm."

"Anyone could dream a storm the night before a ship journey in January!" Edmund snapped.

"And the book going overboard."

Edmund turned and started to walk away. "Tell the bishop your confession, Hunred, I don't care!"

"That's what I should have done, told him beforehand! But I didn't believe! I didn't think I could possibly have foreknowledge, when Abbot Eadred had nothing. But I was wrong, I was wrong! God doesn't choose us because we're worthy. I had the dream, and I didn't take it to Eadred and the bishop because I was a coward, you're right, I was a coward, and too proud and afraid they would tell me I was a fool."

"Who cares?" said Edmund. "I didn't need a dream to see it was wrong, but they didn't want to hear it from me. Maybe they would have believed you and your dream. But I don't care. You made Aelfleda a promise, and *she* believed you, so she gave up everything she could have had!"

And this time he did walk away.

chapter nineteen

THE NEXT MORNING BEGAN WITH THE SINGING OF the monks. Edmund woke from a half-remembered dream in which Derwin was still alive, challenging him to a race from the monastery gate to Lindesfarne hall. Edmund struggled up from the ground in the small camp of the bearers, partway between the monks and the layfolk, groaning and stretching his battered limbs.

Banked fires were being stirred to life throughout the camp, a last hot breakfast of oats cooking in many iron pots, including one that Stitheard was tending.

"Well, now, Edmund," he said, "since you are awake, you can take the ox down to the burn to water him—it's starting to get light now. He's tied to that chestnut tree over there. But have a care—that animal isn't a good heart like Lindo!"

Edmund untied the animal and clucked to encourage him along; despite Stitheard's warning, it came with him more than eagerly. Edmund couldn't help noticing the creature's ribs showed rather more than Lindo's had.

He was halfway to the burn when Caris emerged from the still grayness on his right. "I've been waiting to see you," she said abruptly.

Edmund jumped, and she smirked at catching him out. The ox lowed impatiently, and Edmund clutched the rope tighter as he resumed his tramp toward the burn. "Have you nothing to do besides lie in wait for me?" he said, letting his irritation show … and telling himself he was *not* particularly glad to see her.

"I came here," she said haughtily, "to bring back your cloak, and take my own back."

Edmund pulled back on the lead of the protesting ox till it halted. One-handed, he tried to undo his cloak pin, failing until Caris sniffed and took the rope from him. He let it go grudgingly, and took off the cloak. Without it, the pre-dawn air was clammy; he would be glad of his own longer garment.

Caris dropped the rope to unfasten his cloak from her shoulders, and when he objected said, "Oh, don't fuss! I've seen that ox taken to drink every morning at this camp, and he knows where it is, let him go." She gave the ox a nudge in the flank, and it went ahead with a little snort.

They exchanged the cloaks. "Thank you for the loan," Edmund said, not very graciously. As he fastened his own cloak about him again, he couldn't help but notice the wool was soft to the touch, and sweetly scented with lavender—under the smell of campfire smoke, anyway. "You rinsed the salt out of it in fresh water," he said.

"Yes, Ed, I did," she said smugly. "And I made you a hazelnut cake, too." She handed him a little linen-wrapped packet. "I picked hazelnuts in the woods last fall at Aelfsdene, and saved them till now. I traded some of them at Workington hall the other day for an egg and flour and honey."

"Oh—thank you." He looked, bemused, at the packet and then at her. "No one but Derwin ever called me Ed."

Her features softened ever so slightly. "I know. He used to speak of you to me that way."

"I had a dream about him this morning. About us being home on Lindesfarne." Putting the packet in his belt pouch, Edmund turned toward the burn, and she fell in beside him.

They reached the bank and caught up with the ox, which had waded in a little way and was drinking contentedly. "So," Caris said, "about this promise your brother made to Aelfleda . . ."

"I just finished telling Hunred last night that he was no kin of mine," Edmund spat.

She cocked her head to one side, brows raised. "Really?" Her tone was sincere, not the sarcastic voice she used so often.

"Are you surprised? I'm not like Hunred. I never wanted to be a monk and never will. Come on now, Ox," he called, leaning out over the water and reaching for the ox's lead, but missing. He could think of nothing he wanted less than to get his shoes wet again. He whistled and whickered, but it looked dumbly at him and then gazed about as if taking in the scenery.

Caris said, "So if I wanted *you* to make that promise to *me*, you wouldn't ever break it?"

Edmund's head snapped around, the ox forgotten. "What?"

She drew herself up, hands on hips and pressing her lips together. Fixing her eyes coldly on him she said, "If you think I'm fickle for saying such things when Derwin is little more than a year dead, I'm not! I'm loyal as, as—well, I'm loyal and nothing but! You know, Ed, I might have stayed with Osbert. But I didn't . . . mostly because of Saint Cuthbert."

Caris was never one for a particular show of piety. But Edmund believed in her claim to loyalty. "Because of Abbot

Eadred saving us from the wolf on Doddington moor?"

"Yes. But I'm not like your brother either, Edmund. Maybe I would have been a nun if the bishop had found me a place before the Danes came. But I don't think I ever really wanted that."

The ox wandered across the burn and began cropping some of the grasses on the other side. Edmund frowned at it; it looked like wet shoes for him after all to fetch it back.

Caris was waiting. It was hard to meet her bright eyes. He took a deep breath. "I can't promise, Caris. I'm sworn to be a saint-bearer. I won't ask any girl to wait for some new home we may never have."

Caris folded her arms. "Pea-brain! *You* aren't asking me—*I'm* asking you!" She stood there, eyes narrowed but a half-smirk on her lips. Which Edmund was not, *was not* going to kiss, even though she was making him laugh, and the laughing felt good . . . though why anyone should feel good when a girl was calling him a pea-brain he could not have said.

But the laugh ended, and Edmund looked down as Caris's ghost of a smile began to slip. "I have to get that ox back," he mumbled.

A short silence. Then Caris said, "Well. I have to get back to camp."

"Yes." Edmund nodded, still avoiding looking at her. As she was avoiding looking at him, he knew, or she would have said, "Edmund son of Tida, you look at me!"

Instead she said, "You should come see your mother. She kept hoping you and Hunred would come to the lay camp last night."

Guilt panged in Edmund. "We—the bearers—we were all troubled by what happened, Caris . . ."

She clucked her tongue and said, "That's no excuse!" in her

old voice, which made it feel safe to look at her again. "Edmund, are you so stupid as not to think of how she lost her husband to the sea, and yesterday thought she had lost both her sons to it as well?"

"I—I'm sorry," he said. He *hadn't* thought, not at all!

Caris shook her head, wrinkling her nose. The light had grown enough now that he could see the freckles scattered there, like small flowers across a meadow. "Hunred would never think, of course, but I expected better of *you*, Edmund!"

That barb went home, and she knew it, looking away as his mouth dropped open. He closed it again, clenching his teeth. "I'm not Hunred, Caris. But I'm not Derwin either."

"Derwin would have expected better of you too," she said, and he could not deny it. His stomach knotted as the anger flooded through him.

"All right," he bit out. "Tell her I'll ask leave to come see her when we make camp tonight. I'll make Hunred come too."

"Good." With no word of farewell she turned to start across the pasture in the new pink dawn light.

"Caris!" said Edmund, and she turned, a sullen look on her face. "I was going to say, if there was any girl I *would* promise, it would be you. But I don't want to be compared to Derwin for the rest of my days!"

She gasped, and he was immediately sorry he had said it. Tears gleamed suddenly in her eyes. Edmund panicked. "And don't go crying! I am not going to kiss you again just because you cry!"

Her mouth gaped wider and more indignant still, and she shoved him hard on the arm, bruising it anew. Then she whirled about and stalked swiftly away toward the camp.

Edmund stood wrestling with his impulse to call out to her

again and say he was sorry, to run up and catch her by the arm and spin her about to face him . . . but she was crying, what would he do about it . . . it was probably better to let her go . . .

He sighed as he watched her retreat. Finally he remembered his errand and turned back to the burn.

The ox was nowhere to be seen.

So much for dry shoes. Edmund splashed across the muddy burn, cupped his hands around his mouth, and hollered, "O-OX!" Clambering up the far bank, he scanned in all directions, but no movement in the wild field of tall, seedy thistles and nettles revealed anything, and the contrary beast made no response to his repeated hails.

He found one or two hoofprints near the water, but higher up the bank the ground was harder, and he could not spot any clear trail, upstream or down. If he turned away now to seek help at the camp, the ox could wander still further away.

"Moo—ooo!" he called again. "Here, Ox, here, Ox!"

The sun was now peeping above the wood at the far end of the field, and it came home to Edmund sudden as an earthquake: He had lost the ox, failed in his charge. He was no better, perhaps worse, than Hunred, who had let the Gospel book slip from his fingers. No storm had taken the ox's lead from Edmund—he had let it go of his own will, just because he was talking with a girl.

Edmund groaned and crossed himself. "*Miserere mei, Deus.* Please God, don't let the rest of the company suffer because I have stupidly lost the ox!"

Seek and ye shall find. That was supposed to be about the

kingdom of God and spiritual wisdom, but Brother Trumwin had often quoted it in the schoolroom when one of the
boys mislaid a stylus or a quill. Edmund started pacing the
edge of the field, heading downstream. By the time he reached
the roadside, another thought occurred to him: the ox might
have already recrossed the burn and wandered back toward the
camp on its own. *But if it's gone south in this field or gotten out
to the road or got caught in a thicket up by that wood, the sooner I
find it the better.*

And then he thought he heard something—a rustle up by
the woods. A movement, maybe of a large animal . . . then it
stopped.

He didn't think he could get through the thistle field directly,
so he ran along the road a few rods to where it crossed another
little burn to the south. Wet shoes indeed . . . He made his way
up the burn itself toward the wood. But before he got there, he
found another, less-used road, crossing the water from south
to north. It ran through the overgrown field, veered east, and
plunged into the trees.

Edmund stood looking doubtfully along the pathway. The
oak and ash trees that stood leafless, still awaiting spring, did
not block his immediate view. The early sun was now pouring
through the high bare branches, lighting up the ground, which
was clad in old rotted leaves. The floor of the woodland mounted
gradually into the eastern hills, and the little road quickly bent
away out of sight among them.

Edmund closed his eyes, letting his ears do the searching. A
few sparrows flitting from branch to desolate branch, hardly
peeping. A squirrel digging up a stored acorn in the damp, leafy
ground. Nothing as big as an ox making any sort of sound—

"Cronk!" A raven called from somewhere up ahead. Edmund's

eyes flashed open. That was nothing unusual, a raven in the forest . . .

"Cronk! Cronk!" The raven came nearer.

"Cronk!" Edmund called back. He had never gotten as good as Derwin or Aelfleda at imitating raven sounds. But to his amazement, the black bird swooped swiftly through the branches and perched in an oak tree just inside the entry to the wood.

"Riddle?" Edmund said softly, not daring to hope, and yet . . . Taking a few cautious steps in under the eaves of the wood, Edmund stood just beneath the tree where the raven sat, whistled, and again called, "Riddle!"

The bird cocked its head, hunched its neck to peer down at him. Then without warning it dove down and settled itself on his shoulder as if it had perched there all its life.

"Riddle!" he whispered, hardly daring to believe the bird had escaped and found him across all these miles and after all this time. But it had to be—a wild raven would never come and sit on your shoulder! Carefully he took Caris's hazelnut cake out of the leather bag on his belt, unwrapped it, and broke off a piece to feed the bird. The raven ate it with a little gurgle of pleasure, then rubbed his bill along Edmund's jaw. And at the same moment, Edmund heard the distant low of an ox somewhere well ahead in the woods.

The bird ruffled its feathers, then launched from Edmund's shoulder, winging swiftly ahead along the path.

"Saint Cuthbert!" Edmund whispered, and began to run, heart pounding.

chapter twenty

A S THE ROAD TOOK HIM DEEPER INTO THE FOREST and higher into the hills, a sudden waft of air brought the scent of smoke to his nostrils. *Stop and think, Edmund!* he told himself.

The ox would never have wandered off into the wood like this by itself. Its food was field plants, not hazelnuts and acorns. If Edmund really had heard it lowing somewhere far ahead, it was because someone had seen it in the field and taken it. Who?

"Cronk!" said Riddle, sitting on an overhanging branch a few rods ahead, as if to beckon him on.

The Workington folk were glad to see the haliwerfolc leave, but Edmund thought they would draw the line at stealing outright from a holy company. Danes would just come and wave their swords at you and take what they wanted. Outlaw robbers?

I will not make the mistake I made at Shotton! he vowed, and continued along the road more carefully. He soon heard shouts and conversation, and axe blows. The sounds came from directly ahead. Riddle flitted into the trees to the left, and Edmund whispered, "Good idea, Riddle."

The trees were largely bare here, though Edmund knew the land further upslope would be clad in evergreens. He would have to creep from tree to tree, praying to remain hidden and unheard. Proceeding in this way for some time, he at last saw that the road ended in a wide clearing where a group of some dozen people were at work . . . and hanging from a tree was his ox, strung up dead and ready to be butchered! The people camped around the fire were mostly old men and women, unkempt and not well-looking. A couple of the men had heavy hunting spears. They were speaking English and laughing at their luck in coming across the ox.

An old woman, though, was worriting about the ox's owner. "If it's from Workington, they'll skin us for taking it!"

"Shut your mouth, woman!" said a wiry-haired, gap-toothed man who stood leaning on his spear. "It had no brand, and this side of the burn is Harrington's. If we feed ourselves, our mighty jarl, as he calls himself, won't mind at all if it's from Workington. And Workington dare not molest us, they have an agreement with Harrington for our charcoal."

Then Edmund noticed that the small cooking fire where the old women were huddled was not the main fire; in the middle of the clearing stood a great smoking mound. Charcoal burners, he realized, doing the tedious and exhausting work of making wood into charcoal that would burn hot enough to be used in the blacksmith's forge. The company had now and then met such people in the woods near settlements. Usually they were poor folk, often Wealisc, sometimes slaves being supervised by freemen from a nearby estate. But most of these people in the clearing, Edmund realized from their weapons and well-made but sadly worn clothes, had once been of thegn status. He read the riddle so: They were the remains of the family that had once owned Harrington, to the south of here, and perhaps had never been on good terms with the neighboring Workington. They had been cast out of the hall by a conquering Danish jarl, and were now suffered to live as long as they worked at this wretched labor in the woods.

His heart sank; he couldn't even be angry at them for taking the company's ox. The blame was all his own for losing it.

Riddle called from the far side of the clearing now. The charcoal-burners took no notice. But the worrying woman suddenly spotted Edmund and raised the alarm. The gap-toothed man with the spear blocked his path to the straight road out of the wood. Edmund turned and went instead further into the trees, only to find himself up against a thicket alongside a gurgling burn.

Another man was closing on him from behind, and a third had cut off his escape upstream.

"Wait!" Edmund cried. "The ox isn't from Workington! The owners won't hurt you!"

But the answer he got was cursing and a spear from the man upstream. The man was weak and elderly; his aim and strength failed, and the weapon landed in the leaf mold at Edmund's feet. Without thinking, he snatched it up and found himself facing the whole band. Some of them threw rocks, though he cried again and again for them to listen.

Then the gap-toothed man with the other spear charged at him, and Edmund jogged aside, turned, and ran upstream, elbowing aside the man who had thrown the spear Edmund now clutched. He headed for the more open space east of the charcoal clearing and suddenly came out on the road again, where it continued eastward from the clearing and away into the hills. Cries of "There he goes!" came from the old women by the cooking fire. Edmund set his feet on the road and ran for all he was worth.

BY THE TIME HE FELT HIMSELF SAFE FROM PURSUIT, EDMUND had a new problem: The road had taken him high into the hills amongst the spruce and pine, farther than ever from the company at Workington, with the charcoal-burners still between him and them. To find another way out of the wood would mean turning north and making for the Derwent River, upstream from Workington; but not knowing the land, he could wander for days before ever leaving the trees.

Setting down the spear, he sat down on a fallen tree, mossy and damp in the green gloom, and unwrapped his hazelnut cake again. This brought Riddle down from his perch on a branch above. Edmund shared a little of the dense, nutty cake with the bird and put the rest firmly away.

It started to snow.

He got up again. At all costs he must get down out of the hills before dark. This would take him farther than ever from the company, for he dared not wander in the uncertain country under the branches of the evergreens. There was nothing for it but to continue east on the road, which could not go on forever. He hoped.

This time luck—or Saint Cuthbert—was with him, for the few flakes dissipated, the sky cleared, and the air warmed as he and the raven headed down. The trees became mixed. He crossed a river on a timber bridge, slippery with moss and creaking alarmingly under his feet. But not far past that, as the sun began to wester, he had a view of the valley beyond the wood to the east, and caught sight of a small mere reflecting blue.

Twilight began to obscure the road. Then, through the trees to the south, in the direction of the shore, Edmund saw the red-gold flicker of a campfire in the evening dimness. At the same moment, he heard the chilling howl of a wolf, and another answering. Riddle cawed disapprovingly and vaulted into the trees above.

Edmund's heart leapt into his throat. Brandishing his spear, he turned at once into the woods to pick his way toward the campfire. Halfway there, he realized at least one of the wolves was in fact on the shore. A horse was neighing in panic, a man was shouting, and the wolf snarling.

Edmund stumbled and dodged his way amongst the dark tree-trunks till he emerged onto the shore, where a young man was darting at a wolf with a sword. A short way along the shore from the fire, a second wolf nipped at the heels of a red horse tethered to a stake beside the water. Edmund nearly cheered when the horse lashed out with its hooves and drew a yelp from the wolf, sending it fleeing along the shore. But then he heard a snarl behind him, and turned just in time to defend himself with his spear against a third wolf.

Edmund had never faced anything bigger than a fish with a spear, so when the wolf leapt at him, all he could think to do was turn the point of the spear toward it and thrust. The savage creature twisted out of the way with a yelp and instantly came at him from the side instead. Hardly knowing what he was doing, Edmund swept the spear around, catching the beast a stunning blow on the ear. It faltered and shook its head.

In that moment, the man with the sword jumped forward

with a terrifying yell, swung his blade two-handed over his head and brought it down on the wolf's neck, severing it cleanly. Edmund leapt back, heart racing.

The swordsman lifted his blade high in triumph, shouting a wordless victory cry to the darkening sky. It echoed through the bowl of the mere and hills round about, and his horse, still tethered by the water, snorted as if in agreement.

Silence fell again, and Edmund drew a shuddering breath. The swordsman turned to face him. He looked like some kind of rough hero, all right, with his bloody sword and his worn tunic and cloak, tall and seemingly well-featured in the firelight, his eyes intense and his dark hair hanging unkempt around his face and shoulders, a slight beard on his jaws.

"Waes hal," Edmund said at last. The warrior nodded at him and went to clean his blade. Edmund saw by the light of the fire that the remaining wolf lay dead near the shore. The swordsman rinsed his blade in the water and dried it on his cloak before sheathing it, then dragged the wolf carcass over to the other. "I claim the pelts," he said, "since I did the killing. But you can share the meat and my camp for tonight."

"Thank you," said Edmund. "I'll make some roasting sticks." Wolf wasn't something anyone would normally eat, but in the last three years he had seen people hungry enough to eat plenty of strange things.

As he stood up and drew his own belt knife to cut and sharpen sticks, Riddle swept down on the severed wolf head with a cackle of glee. The swordsman cried, "Yah!" and swatted at the bird, but Edmund cried, "No!"

"He's with me," he explained, and the swordsman stared as Riddle settled again on the wolf's head, muttering, and began to peck at the eyes.

"My name is Edmund, son of Tida," said Edmund.

The swordsman looked at him and nodded. "Godfrith." He went back to his horse to release it from the stake, speaking soothingly and coiling up the rope. He looped the horse's reins around a branch, and got Edmund to help him use the rope to string up the first wolf carcass for skinning.

Edmund cut some suitable small branches and came back to sharpen them while he watched Godfrith work. He began at the top and worked the pelt down off the carcass. "I've never seen that. It looks a deal more trouble than cleaning fish."

"The pelt without the head will be worth a lot less," said Godfrith, glancing at Riddle. The raven continued to enjoy the severed wolf head.

"Where will you trade the pelts? Where are you headed?" Edmund asked.

Godfrith gave him an appraising look. "We meet in troubled days, as two strangers in the wilderness. Is it time yet for such trust?"

Edmund had noticed that his companion gave no ancestral names, just his own. Perhaps he was an outlaw? "We just fought off wolves together," said Edmund, as he began cutting strips of meat from the hanging carcass and threading them onto his sharpened sticks. "What more do you want? I'll tell you everything about me first, if you feel better that way. I'm a fisherman's son from Lindesfarne. I left there four winters ago with the whole company and the body of Holy Cuthbert himself, for fear of the Danes. We've wandered all over Northumbria. I was a messenger for Bishop Eardwulf, and now I'm one of the seven saint-bearers. Only I stupidly lost our ox at Workington, and I ran from the people who stole it, and now I don't know how to get back to the company. I can tell you more, but that's the gist."

Godfrith said, "We'll eat now, skin the second one in the morning," and they put the meat-sticks over the fire.

They ate in silence, chewing the tough meat repeatedly. It was odd and rank, but Edmund could not deny he felt better for it. They cut and ate a second and then a third batch of meat strips, knowing it wouldn't keep. But at last they wanted no more, washed in the mere, and put some more wood on the fire. Riddle, likewise sated, came to Edmund's shoulder and prepared to roost for the night.

After a while, Godfrith said, "My father left me hostage, and he was killed in the fighting. His friends took me back, but treated me as little more than a slave. So I set out on my own. Some day, I will find friends of my own. And I will make those false friends sorry they did such things to their lord's son."

He did not look at Edmund, but stared into the fire, as if seeing again the scenes of injustice he had known.

After a moment, Edmund said, "I wish you well. And I thank you for killing the wolves and sharing the meat with me."

A small smile quirked the corner of Godfrith's mouth, and he nodded to Edmund in acknowledgement. They sat in silence again for a while—even Edmund was too tired to talk, and at last he curled up in his cloak facing the fire and closed his eyes while Riddle complained about having to shift his perch. The smell of camp smoke and roast meat enveloped him, and the last thing his ears took in was Godfrith's low humming of a rhythmic, unfamiliar tune.

chapter twenty-one

THE SUN WAS ALREADY HIGH AND GLEAMING OFF THE surface of the mere when Edmund woke to find strips of cooked wolf meat lying on a rock by the fire. Raising himself on one elbow, he glanced about. The headless wolf skin hung on some branches stuck in the ground on the other side of the fire. The horse still stood with its reins looped about a tree branch, and Godfrith was just peeling the pelt of the second wolf down off the hind legs. Edmund jumped up.

"I was going to help with that!" he protested.

Godfrith glanced over his shoulder at him. "I don't need help."

Edmund could hardly speak for a moment. Maybe he was too used to traveling with the company all these years, where everyone pitched in with everything. Or maybe Godfrith was too used to being alone, having no one else to share work and rest, joy and trouble . . .

"But—I need to help," Edmund insisted.

That appeared to startle Godfrith. He turned to face Edmund

in the morning light, which now revealed a surprising scar that ran downwards from one temple, across his nose and opposite cheek. After a moment he nodded and said, "All right—cut some more of this meat while I clean the pelt. I want to cook as much as we can carry, it'll keep better."

Before long they were eating again, with still more meat skewered over the fire, the second pelt scraped as clean as could be managed and laid out, and Riddle picking the bones clean. Even the horse was content, tethered by the rope to a stake again and wandering the waterside cropping grass. Edmund was not so hungry as last night, and his meat grew cold while he talked about where he had been and how he didn't even know which way the company had planned to go.

But Godfrith said nothing. Why was he so reticent? Finally Edmund said, "You remind me of a friend I had. He didn't talk a lot either." And then tales of Derwin and Riddle and races on Lindesfarne poured out of him like a spate of spring melt water overflowing the banks of a burn.

The torrent ceased, and Edmund bit into his last strip of meat.

Godfrith observed, "No wonder your friend was quiet. You talk enough for two."

Edmund nearly choked. But then he saw the smile tugging at the corner of Godfrith's mouth, and the glint in his eyes. Blushing, Edmund swallowed the chunk of meat. "Ha. That sounds like another friend of mine. Well, she isn't really a friend, she's a girl."

This time Godfrith laughed out loud. Edmund sighed and changed the subject. "Do you know this country at all? I have to go back to Workington and start looking for my people."

"You can come with me," said Godfrith. "Cockermouth is

the place to sell these pelts. We'll get there easily by dark."

Edmund warmed to the invitation. "Cockermouth, yes, where the Cocker River flows into the Derwent—we passed through it on the way to Workington. Maybe the company has even passed through already, if they are going east or north!"

Godfrith gathered the remaining cooked meat and got up to put it in his saddle bag. "This little tarn feeds into the Cocker River. We cross the river and follow the road on the east bank, north past Lorton."

And with that word *tarn*, suddenly Edmund knew him. They were on the shores of a *mere* or a *water*—but in Danske tunga it was called a *tarn*. Take away the scar, the shaggy hair and strug-gling beard, the height and breadth gained in the last year, and Godfrith was revealed as the translator from Shotton.

I talk too much, Edmund thought in chagrin. *Always. But does he not recognize me too?*

Godfrith finished securing the pelts behind the saddle and swung himself up. "You said you were a runner. Can you keep up, once we make the road, if I trot my horse at an easy jog?"

"Yes, no trouble at all," said Edmund, kicking dirt on the campfire. *And he is being so careful not to even tell me the* horse's *name!*

Godfrith started north along the shore, and Edmund whis-tled for Riddle. Tucking the spear under his arm with a prayer to Saint Cuthbert, he followed along behind.

AT AN INN IN THE BUSY RIVER PORT OF COCKERMOUTH THAT evening, they traded the remaining wolf-meat for a bed and soup and bread. An evening around the central hearth at the inn revealed no news of the company. Worry about their where-abouts and puzzlement about Godfrith gnawed at Edmund's mind long after the fire burned low and all the guests settled down onto the straw mattresses placed around the walls of the open hall.

In the morning they went to sell the spear at the smithy. God-frith stood by, giving the smith an evil eye until he gave Edmund a fair price—nowhere near compensation for the lost ox, but it should feed him for a few days. Edmund then went along to watch Godfrith haggle with a tanner over the wolf pelts. When the deal was done, Godfrith stepped through the mud with a smug look on his face. "That price was better than I hoped. Come back to the inn and drink with me before you head to Workington."

"So you aren't headed that way yourself?" Edmund asked.

Godfrith hesitated. "I wasn't. But—this story about the saint. A whole company is carrying the relics about?"

"Bishop Eardwulf is leading us. Monks and layfolk, old and young. But everywhere we go, we fear the heathen Danes."

They walked on across the busy market. Godfrith, silent again now, stopped to look idly at some wooden bowls. After a moment, Edmund dared to say, "Why not come and meet the bishop? Wherever you're going," he took a deep breath, "you could pray before the relics of Saint Cuthbert."

When Godfrith gave him a cautious look, he hastened to add, "You don't have to tell me what your business is. I know that . . . well, after all, these are dangerous times . . ."

Godfrith put back the bowl he had been handling. "I'll tell you . . . the truth is, I am looking for allies." His voice dropped, and he leaned closer. "I give you my word, though I keep my business quiet, I am not about anything dishonorable."

"I didn't think—"

Suddenly Godfrith's jaw slackened and his eyes widened as he stared across the market ground. Edmund followed his gaze and saw a pair of armed men, who spotted Godfrith at the same time. Edmund had the barest of moments to realize that the tall red-headed one was familiar to him—Frana, son of Thorstein!

Godfrith gripped Edmund's arm. "If I'm not back at the inn tonight, take care of my horse!" Then he turned and ran, dodging women crying strings of fish for sale and children playing at tag amongst the stalls.

"Yah!" cried Frana, and his partner began shouting in Danske. They came thundering across the marketplace, sending chickens squawking as they ran. Without a thought, Edmund stuck out a foot, and Frana went down cursing; Edmund ducked out of sight behind the woodwork stall before he could be seen.

The whole market was turned upside down as Godfrith fled the men. Peeking round the far corner of the stall, Edmund saw the second man run smack into a pottery stall as Godfrith jumped over a passing goat and ran on toward the road. The man stumbled on, joined by Frana, leaving the potter cursing and demanding payment. But Godfrith pulled away from his pursuers quickly, dashing across the road and into the woods. Edmund gaped in admiration: Now that was what he called a runner!

After a while the market settled down. Edmund bought some dried apples and went back to the inn, where he went to the stable and fed one of them to the horse. He wished Godfrith had told him its name, but at least it didn't bite him. He had no appetite himself. He kept hearing Derwin's cry, and the sickening thunk of Frana's sword striking him . . .

Edmund was too disturbed now to spend the day sitting about the inn. He paid the master of the inn a penig, saying that he and his friend would be staying another night, and went out to stroll about, keeping his eyes open for the warriors. Neither they nor Godfrith reappeared. The strolling did nothing to relieve his anxiety, nor did a run down the road as far as the next little estate and back. He came into the inn again at sunset, sweaty and agitated.

And there he saw Frana and the other warrior sitting by the hearth, drinking and talking loudly in their language. Edmund slipped quietly into his own place. He didn't think they had noticed him enough to recognize him as the one who had tripped Frana, or that he had been talking to Godfrith when they spotted him. Edmund wondered belatedly, *Have I changed as much as Godfrith in the last year? Will Frana remember me from Shotton?* He kept in the shadows by the wall, hoping not to find out.

He accepted a bowl of leek-and-onion broth from the innmaster's wife and sopped it up with chewy fresh bread. A traveling harper performed a few light tunes for the inn's company and sent around a bowl for payment. Edmund put in one of his dried apples. The two Danes, though, frowned.

Frana spoke—to Edmund's surprise, in English still heavily accented but now more fluent than it had been a year ago at Shotton: "You, singer. Why you sing not one of *our* songs?"

"It will be my honor to learn if you will teach me," said the musician, with a bow, a flourish on his harp, and the winning smile that performers who earn their bread by their art learn to use. "Come, sing—I will pluck a note or two as you do!"

Frana's companion guffawed, and others in the company urged him on, so he stood up.

"This song is called *Havamal*. It is Odin's traveling wisdom song. It is long. I sing only a little."

"You *know* only little!" his friend mocked him, and the company laughed.

Frana began to sing. His voice was not very fine, but before long Edmund recognized the tune he had heard Godfrith humming by the mere. Some of the other folk present were also humming along now, by which Edmund realized that several of them were in fact Danes. When Frana finished, his partner stood up and spoke in English:

Young and alone on a long road,
Once I lost my way:
Rich I felt when I found another;
Man rejoices in man.

The translation wakened afresh the loneliness that had come over Edmund in the woods after he escaped the charcoal burners. Heathen the song might be, but it spoke true.

When the inn began to settle down, Edmund went out to the stable to check on the horse again. *I'll have to take it with me to Workington in the morning,* he thought. *I hardly know a thing about riding. Saint Cuthbert help me!*

The instant he opened the stable door, the prayer was answered. Godfrith was saddling his horse by lantern light. He looked up in alarm at the opening of the door, but like a shallow writing on the sand erased by surf, the alarm gave way to relief when he saw it was Edmund.

"Godfrith, they're in the inn—the men who chased you!" said Edmund.

"I feared they might be. I'm leaving as soon as the moon rises. Did you pay for tonight's stay? Including me and my horse?"

"Well, yes, but—"

"I've paid off the stable boy," Godfrith said, gesturing with a tilt of his head toward the loft. "He's asleep on wine up there."

He rummaged in the pouch at his belt and produced a silver *stycca*. "Here."

"That's far more than I paid!" Edmund protested.

"Take it. For helping me, if you like."

Edmund looked at him sharply. "No, thank you. We have helped each other, and that is good. I don't know why you are looking for allies, but you can't buy my friendship."

Edmund had never imagined that Godfrith's subtle countenance could show such a stricken expression. "I never meant to! Look, you'll need the money. If we have the luck to meet again, you can return it."

Edmund looked at him for a moment. He seemed sincere. "If we are friends, you'll trust me with the truth of who you are."

Godfrith replied steadily. "Yes, I will. We've met before, though you have failed to recognize me, Edmund son of Tida."

Edmund grinned. "No, I didn't entirely, translator. But you've gotten to look pretty rough since Shotton."

"Ah." Godfrith smiled ruefully. "The scar, yes—I had a closer escape from some of Thorstein's men some weeks ago. Look at this." Setting the coin atop the stall divider, Godfrith drew his sword and held the hilt toward Edmund. There on the top of the round pommel, the lantern light gleamed off the small, familiar cross of inlaid jet.

"Derwin's sword!"

Godfrith sheathed the sword. "Yes. And this is the horse I took the day we escaped Thorstein. He was my father's. I would give you back your friend's sword now, Edmund, but it's the only one I have, and I need it." He took the coin down and held it out again to Edmund. "If we meet again and have both prospered, you will give me my silver and I will give you the sword. Are we agreed?"

After a moment, Edmund nodded and accepted the coin, putting it into his own pouch. "But tell me one thing—why you thought of seeking an ally in Bishop Eardwulf?"

"There is no Dane or Angle where honor are concerned," said Godfrith. "My father was one of the great army that came to find land here in Northumbria. He and his band fought a noble fight with the English lord of an estate. They called an end to their fighting and made a peace agreement to divide the estate, and I was given as hostage and foster son to that Angle lord, while my father went away with Thorstein and his other friends to fight in Halfdan's army in Ireland. My father died in the fighting."

"I'm sorry," said Edmund. "I lost my father to the sea."

Godfrith nodded. "I lost a second father when that English lord died of illness that winter. His widow was a mother to me, but then after Halfdan died, Thorstein came back and took me from her. I have freed myself from Thorstein and mean to take my place among the lords of this land."

"A place that was an Angle's once," Edmund pointed out.

Godfrith shook his head and shrugged. "It was some Wealisc lord's place before any Angle's. People make war, it's the way of the world."

"It isn't the way of the kingdom of God. Or the company of Cuthbert," said Edmund.

"I know. That's why I wish to befriend your bishop. The Danes about Jorvik and by the Tyne have not agreed on a new leader, but there is no thegn of the Northumbrians to fight them either. It's time we settled, Angle and Dane both under one rule in Northumbria. But I can't come to your bishop today. I will return to the hills, by ways Thorstein's men don't know. Edmund, if they happen to realize you were with me, you will be in danger on the road."

"I know. Now you've got your horse, I'll go to the landing tonight, and find a boat heading for Derwentmouth tomorrow."

"So you *will* need that coin, for your passage." Godfrith grinned. "Good luck now, Edmund!"

Edmund smiled back. "God go with you, Godfrith."

Then they doused the lantern and went out of the stable under the stars, each on his separate way.

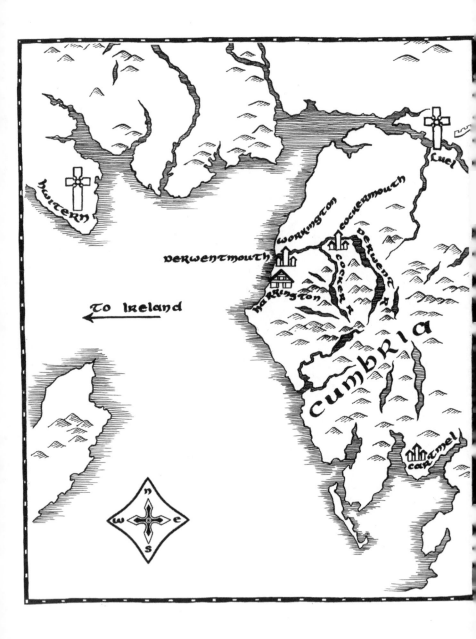

hartern

Cuel

workington

cockermouth

derwentmouth

cocken r.

derwent r.

warrington

To Ireland

cumbria

carmel

N
W E
S

Part III

Near Hwitern

A.D. 882

chapter twenty-two

EDMUND STOOD WATCHING THE TIDE WORK ITS WAY far out into the bay while Franco and Stitheard sat in the sunny meadow nearby, trying to repair a sad little bit of harness. Edmund still felt guilty at times about the lost ox, two years gone now. Ever since, the bearers themselves had drawn the cart, rigging the leather for man instead of beast. One bad crop year had followed another, and not for love or money could the company get themselves a new animal of any kind.

The day he parted from Godfrith at Cockermouth and found a boatman to take him downriver to Workington, Edmund had begun a wretched and lonely quest to rejoin the company. Only after making his way south along the coast for days with no news of them did he reach the reluctant conclusion that they had taken the same forest road that had previously led him to the Harrington coal burners and beyond to the mere where he met Godfrith. Trying to catch up to them, he felt like a dog chasing its own tail. Dodging Danes among the hills and meres, and his own countrymen at every settlement suspicious of a lone wanderer, he drifted for weeks before he at last found any news of the haliwerfolc. Only the company of Riddle kept him from stark despair. Hungry, lonely, and afraid, he at last caught up with them at Easter, at Cartmel deep in the south of Cumbria. From there the company had eventually wandered further northward again by inland roads, always moving on when they found they had worn out their welcome.

Now on this windy May morning, a way up the coast from Hwitern, the farthest place north they had yet settled at for more than a week at a time, the memory of that day of reunion warmed him still. Remembering Caris's rebuke, he had humbled himself utterly to his mother, and was glad to see her joy. Even Hunred had thumped him on the back, though the two of them had avoided looking at each other. And Caris had kissed him—only on the cheek, but in front of everyone, so that his face went hot at all the cheers.

"Look how far that tide is going out!" said Edmund. "That's well beyond anything I've seen it do in all the weeks we've been on these shores."

Stitheard the landsman grunted, uninterested. "We'll be moving on again in a few days, the bishop says."

Edmund's brief surge of spirit deflated. They had lost members who scattered in hard times, and a few died in the harsh winters. When they came in desperation to isolated Hwitern, the ancient home of a saint older than Cuthbert called Ninian, they found that the monastery and settlement destroyed by Halfdan's raiders years ago was now being built up by new settlers—Northmen from Ireland.

"But you know," said Franco, trying to salvage the mood from the glum Stitheard, "these Northmen are Christians now, not like the Danes. Even though they have their own ways from

Ireland. I know they don't care for us because of that, but maybe there's some hope—"

"Look around you," Stitheard growled. "The Hwitern folk are just scraping by like everyone else. Yes, there's some fish to eat, but with bad harvests and sickness these past years, it's all they can do to feed themselves. No one has time or money to build churches or new homes for strangers like us."

Just then, Hunred came pounding over the sheep-cropped turf. "I've had a vision! I've seen Saint Cuthbert!"

The others turned to look at him in astonishment.

Franco, who knew him better than anyone, said doubtfully, "Hunred . . . how long have you been fasting now?"

Hunred did look wild, and maybe a little flushed. Since rejoining the company, Edmund found himself a little more able to tolerate Hunred, and now he felt compelled to say in fairness, "He did have a prophetic dream once before, though."

Hunred gave him a grateful look. "It's true. The saint spoke to me! We can find the Gospel book again in this very low tide. You have to go down on the sands and start looking!"

Stitheard shook his head, frowning. "My boy, I think you have a fever." Stitheard still called the three of them "boy," though they all of them had young beards on their chins now.

"Just do it, Stitheard—if you don't, the *bishop* will tell you to do it after I speak to him. Edmund, you come with me—there's something else I have to tell you. Franco, go on!"

<hr />

WHEN THEY HAD SEEN THE BISHOP AND HE AGREED TO SEND the monks out to search the sands, Hunred led Edmund on his mysterious second errand.

"There's a horse," said Hunred. "I saw it in the vision. Somewhere about the trees along the burn, it's wandering. A red horse," he said, and he was shouting in his excitement now, "and a bridle is hanging on a tree branch. Cuthbert said so!"

Edmund continued in Hunred's wake, utterly bemused.

"And there it is!" Hunred whistled, pointing at a fine coppery horse nibbling at the young leaves of the willows that skirted the spring-chuckling water. The horse lifted its head curiously.

"Cronk! Cronk!" Riddle flew up from a tree nearby and came to Edmund's shoulder. The raven rubbed his beak along Edmund's jaw, then immediately returned to his perch again.

"I see the bridle!" said Edmund, and dashed forward to fetch it down from the branch where Riddle sat proudly. He handed it to Hunred, who called to the horse and held the bridle up for it to see. The horse trotted over willingly and let the leather be put onto it.

"This can't be right," Edmund said, shaking his head. "A horse escaped and wandering from afar I might believe, but the bridle being here—that has to mean the owner is near, Hunred."

Hunred stroked the horse's neck, awe on his face. "If the owner shows himself, I will tell him Saint Cuthbert claims this horse for his own."

"Hunred, what if the owner is a heathen Dane? He'll call you a horse thief and kill you!"

Hunred's strangely lit eyes met Edmund's. "Don't you see— this is redemption, for both of us! The Gospel book I lost overboard will be found on the sands, and Cuthbert has sent us a horse to replace the ox that escaped you at Workington. Come, horse," he said, face aglow, and led the animal off without a look back at Edmund.

Riddle flew back to Edmund's shoulder, and he stroked the

raven's glossy feathers absently as he watched Hunred leading the horse back across the field. The bird squawked.

"Come on, Riddle," said Edmund. "We'd better see if the horse's owner is about. Maybe it'll be all right if we explain that Hunred's fevered, and get the bishop to give the horse back. Halloo!" he called out to the trees. "Anyone about?"

No answer. And then Riddle flew at one of the trees, scolding.

A dark-haired figure stepped out from behind a trunk. "Well, I am found out, it seems."

The beard was a little fuller, the shoulders perhaps broader than two years ago, but Edmund could not mistake the shrewd glint in the eyes. "Godfrith!" They slapped one another on the back, laughing, while Riddle chortled on his branch above.

"I didn't know it was you at first," said Godfrith. "When I saw two men running this way and shouting—I thought it best to keep out of sight."

"That was my mad brother Hunred, who thinks your horse is a gift from Saint Cuthbert." Edmund rolled his eyes.

"Well, he's almost right—it's a gift *for* Saint Cuthbert. I left the bridle on that branch, letting him run free for the last time before he has to pull your saint's cart. If you'd looked a little further under the trees, you'd have seen my saddle there too."

"You knew the company was here?"

"I've been in this north country a while now. Fighting the Picts. Edmund, if we don't unite Angle and Dane in Northumbria soon, I think those Picts will gather themselves together and come pouring down on us all from the north like a great storm wave."

"Bishop Eardwulf says much the same."

"And I've killed Thorstein."

Edmund didn't know what to say. Once, he would have been glad to hear of the death of any Dane. And Thorstein, of them all—along with his son Frana and his other man—was the Dane responsible for Derwin's death. But now here was God-frith. He was a Dane, and he was also a friend. Edmund didn't like to think of him with blood on his hands.

"Let's sit," said Edmund.

Godfrith agreed. They found a dry spot in the pasture and continued.

"Since the day we left Cockermouth," Godfrith told him, "I've been traveling about, making friends here and there about the lands north of the Tyne. Some of them English friends, as well as Danes."

> Young and alone on a long road,
> Once I lost my way:
> Rich I felt when I found another;
> Man rejoices in man,

Edmund recited, and grinned at the astonished expression on Godfrith's face. "Frana sang it at the inn that night, and the other Dane with him translated it."

"My father made me learn it by heart when I was only small," said Godfrith. "But I hope I have been more fortunate in my friends than he was in his. After Cockermouth, I went north and joined a band of Dane warriors who set out to warn the Picts off our Northumbrian lands . . . and it turned out Thorstein was among them. He accused me of horse-stealing; I told the others the truth, that it was my father Hardacnut's horse and rightly mine. We fought it out, and Thorstein lost. I so impressed the men in that company that now I have a war-band of twenty men ready to call me their jarl."

Coming from most men, it would sound like boasting, but from Godfrith it was a simple statement of truth. He looked like a jarl now, Edmund thought. Bronze rings circled his arms and a silver pin fastened his cloak on his shoulder. The cloak was woven in the fine black-and-white checked pattern most favored among the people in the north.

"But is Frana still after you, then? To avenge his father?"

"If he is, he's biding his time. He doesn't frighten me." Godfrith grinned wolfishly.

"So now, you are ready to meet the bishop and make him one of your allies too?" Edmund guessed.

Godfrith nodded. "I'm on my way back to Whittingham, where I was fostered. I have friends among the English thegns round about there. My men and I are camped today at a place to the east, on the far side of this bay. I hear those Irish-Northmen who hold Hwitern did not welcome you. I didn't want to provoke them by riding into their country with an armed company."

"They have their own Irish priest. He finds us suspect. They claim this land and tolerate us here, some miles away from their main settlement. We've been living on shellfish from the sands of the bay here, mostly."

"I come as a pilgrim, with my horse as a friendship gift for the saint's people. Sigr's a bit middle-aged now, so I've found myself a faster mount, but he is still strong and useful."

"You know," said Edmund, "I can't give your silver stycca back. I managed not to spend it for months while I scraped by, trying to catch up with the company. When I met them again, I handed it to the purser. It's long since been spent for food for the company."

"Well, I'm sorry I can't give your friend's sword back just yet, Edmund—I carry a better one now," he said, touching the hilt of the weapon at his side. "I've saved the other for you, though—it's at Whittingham with my foster-mother. But as for your bishop—I've come to tell him that one day, when I have my own lands and a place in the counsels of the lords of Northumbria, I will build a church to Saint Cuthbert, and do all I can to help your people find a new home."

Edmund stood up. "Many a lord has promised us a church for our saint—when times get better. But I believe you are a man who keeps promises, Godfrith."

Godfrith got to his feet as well. "A promise made is a fish in the net. A promise kept is the fish cooked and eaten." He grinned, and Edmund laughed in return.

"Very well. Let's find the bishop."

Godfrith fetched his saddle, and Riddle flew on ahead of them toward the bay. As they topped the gentle rise of the pasture where it looked downslope, they found a wild scene upon the sands below. Edmund had never in his life expected to see Hunred being hoisted like a battle hero upon the shoulders of the bearers, while the sober monks of Lindesfarne shouted and cheered. Hunred held up a square, dark object.

"What's all this?" Godfrith wondered.

"The Book," said Edmund, struck with awe. The bishop and Abbot Eadred were there now as well. "It's the Gospel Book we lost overboard at Derwentmouth. It's a miracle."

"Your brother thought my horse a miracle."

"Abbot Eadred says that coincidences are just *quiet* miracles. But Godfrith, if that really is the Book—and if it is not utterly ruined from the sea—then that is a sure miracle, loud and clear!"

The monks began to sing *Non nobis, Domine*.

"My English foster-mother at Whittingham taught me my

letters," said Godfrith. "But I don't know much Latin. What is the song?"

"A psalm. It begins, 'Not unto us, O Lord, but to Your Name give glory.'"

Hunred was lowered again, and now the bishop was carrying the sea-ravaged package at the head of a procession, the singers falling into two orderly lines.

"Come with me." With his left hand Edmund took Godfrith by the arm, and with his right made the sign of the cross. When the procession approached, Edmund took his place among the bearers, bringing Godfrith alongside.

On reaching the camp, Bishop Eardwulf and Abbot Eadred carried the book into the tent sheltering the holy coffin, and the bearers were not forbidden to come in and gather round the body of their saint while the box was laid on top. Edmund, full of conviction, took the saddle from Godfrith and set it aside, then drew him along into the solemn place, dimly lit by one lantern hanging from the roof-pole. No one made free to interrupt the bishop's prayers to ask who this stranger might be, to dare approach the holy relics at this most holy moment. Godfrith made the sign of the cross like all the others.

The bishop ended his prayer, and the bearers said, "Amen." Then he held out his hand, not taking his eyes from the parcel before him. "A knife."

chapter twenty-three

"Take mine," said Godfrith, stepping forward swiftly to offer the carved silver hilt of a dagger.

The bishop raised his brows, but took the knife and used it to cut the tightly knotted ropes binding the wooden box. Edmund had no doubt it was the same he had secured so carefully onto the ship at Derwentmouth. But what condition were its contents in?

The bishop lifted off the lid of the box and handed it to Eadred. Then he unpacked the unwashed wool clippings and gave those to Hunred. He lifted out the waxed linen packet, tightly bound with hemp string, and set it on the coffin lid beside the box. Murmured prayers and crossings filled the tent as layer after layer of linen and leather and wax came off . . . and then the gold and gems of the Gospel cover emerged flashing into the lantern light from its humble housing, like a royal bride coming out into the sun from some half-ruined churl's hut. The men gasped at the sight.

"Silence, now," said the bishop, and making the sign of the

cross he laid a hand on the metal cover, murmuring a prayer.

Edmund knew that of the bearers, only he had ever seen this glorious treasure, the night Abbot Eadred had shown it to him after Derwin was killed. And he knew that greater treasure still awaited them within the jewel-encrusted cover if... the sea had not taken a toll upon the marvelous embellishments of the Holy Scriptures.

Hands trembling, Bishop Eardwulf opened the cover. Edmund saw again the writhing patterns inked in many colors upon the page. The bearers held their breath as the bishop turned page after page. At last he reached the Gospel of John, which everyone there knew had always been Saint Cuthbert's favorite book, and began to read: "*In principio erat Verbum et Verbum erat apud Deum et Deus erat Verbum.*"

He looked up, and tears glistened on his worn and weary cheeks. "*In the beginning was the Word, and the Word was with God, and the Word was God.* My brothers, we will make a closer examination, but as yet I see no sign that the Holy Pages have taken any harm from the sea. Thanks be to God!"

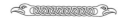

THEY CARRIED THE BOOK OUT TO THE WAITING HALIWERFOLC, who fell to their knees in reverence. The only sound on the hill was the wind, and the gulls crying overhead.

"My brethren," said the bishop, "Look now at the cross upon the cover of the Gospel Book, worked in gems and gold, and see with spiritual eyes. Listen, people of the saint, to the words of the poet Cynewulf, who tells of the cross itself speaking in his dream!" The bishop raised his voice in the rhythmic words of a poem, not in Latin but in their own tongue.

The young Hero Himself ungirded
He that was Almighty God
Strong and stern in spirit.
He climbed upon the towering cross
Courageous before the crowd
Coming to free mankind.

"That is the first time I have heard the Christian God spoken of as a warrior," Godfrith said in Edmund's ear.

The bishop blessed the people with the Gospel book, holding it high and moving it in the sign of the cross. The monks chanted another psalm and the bishop took the book back to Cuthbert's coffin. Eadred dismissed the people, bidding them make merry. Then the bishop beckoned Godfrith and Edmund to come out with him and over to his little hut.

"Edmund, fetch what hospitality you can for our guest from the stores."

Edmund went to the monk who had charge of the stores, and told him this visitor was important enough to breach a certain small cask of mead. The company had been given it at their last stop (as what Stitheard called a "please go away now" present). Then he went to Caris and begged some of her famous hazelnut cakes.

"I gave you three already!" she exclaimed. "And you've eaten them all?"

"But these are for the bishop's special guest," he wheedled, carefully not admitting that he had indeed already finished the ones she had given him. She gave him one of her best frowns, growling at him; but she also gave him the cakes.

By the time he arrived, the bishop and the Dane were deep in conversation. Godfrith looked up from the small table when

Edmund came in with the flask of mead, cakes, and cups.

"You know, Bishop, Edmund here may have saved my life," Godfrith said as the bishop poured.

"What!" said Edmund. "I think it was the other way around!"

Godfrith shook his head. "I made the killing blows. But alone against all three wolves? If you hadn't arrived to distract them, I don't know how it would have turned out."

"Edmund, sit with us," said the bishop.

You had to obey, when the bishop said such a thing, but it felt strange. True, he wasn't a mere boy any more, but he was still the most junior of the bearers. So he sat, but refused the mead, nervous that he would spill it.

"So, Godfrith," said the bishop, giving the visitor a shrewd look over the edge of his mead-cup, "you really think you will become somebody of consequence in the new Northumbria? Do you realize that will only truly be possible if you embrace the Christian faith?"

Godfrith set his cup down. "But I am already baptized. My father Hardacnut agreed to it when he made peace and left me to foster with Lord Wistan of Whittingham. So Wistan's widow, Lady Tola, who now holds his lands, is also my god-mother, you see. I have traveled much, and I can tell you the names and places where you will find at least an open mind among new Dane lords. Bring a scribe here, and I will dictate all the details to him. You will be able to plan a tour and forge bonds of friendship for the future. As for me, I am bound for Jorvik to do the same."

"Where I hear the Danes cannot agree who should be king," said the bishop.

"Have you heard that any Northumbrian Angle is prepared to step forward and lead a rebellion against the Danes now?"

Bishop Eardwulf eyed the young man. Each of them was as hard to read as the other, Edmund thought. But then the bishop said, "No. I believe the time for that is past. Do you know the writings of the Venerable Bede, Godfrith?"

Godfrith shook his head. "I've heard his name."

"He is the historian of all historians among the people of this land. He tells how the Angles and Saxons invaded these shores, ravening heathens who stole away the lands of the Britons who were here before them, the people we call the Wealas. They were Christians, the Wealas—like the Irish Northmen at Hwitern. And do you know what Bede writes about the Wealas? He chides them for not having brought the gospel to their conquerors!"

Godfrith set his head on one side, regarding the bishop with curiosity.

Eardwulf leaned back, slapped his hands on the table, and smiled. "I will not have it written so of the people of Northumbria! Our earthly kingdom is conquered. Come, then, all ye Danes—why stop at an earthly kingdom? Seek the Pearl of Great Price, the kingdom of heaven. Edmund—go fetch a scribe, we will do as our friend Godfrith says!"

To Edmund's delight, when all the scribe work was done, the bishop gave him leave to see Godfrith back to where two of his men awaited him at a crossroads a half mile to the north.

The moment they were on the road, Godfrith said, "They'll be fretting at how long I'm gone, though I told them you were all monks and unarmed. I had best run from here—you needn't come further if you don't want."

Edmund grinned in triumph. "Ha! I'm the fastest man ever born on Lindesfarne. Do you think you can keep up with me?"

Godfrith grinned back. "If we hadn't fought wolves together,

Engel-monn, I would take your ears off with my sword for that boast!"

"Anyone can swing a sword," Edmund mocked. "Even if you did cut off my ears, I could still outrun you!"

"Ha! We'll see, then! Let's jog to that chestnut tree to warm up, and then it's off with no stopping till we meet my men!"

So they loped up the road, easing their muscles into readiness and stopping at the tree. "I challenged," said Edmund. "You can call the start."

"Agreed. On three." They readied themselves, and Godfrith threw Edmund a taunting look, capping it by counting in Danske: "*Ein! Tveir! Thrir!*"

Edmund ran with pleasure, not hurrying to pull ahead of Godfrith, who was longer-legged and fit, but slightly burdened with his sword and traveling cloak. Godfrith kept working his way a little ahead and shooting back a daring look at Edmund. *A mistake, for a racer*, Edmund thought smugly. He refused the bait each time, and Godfrith would fall back even with him again.

Then they came round the edge of a little wood all clad in bright spring green, and Edmund saw two men and three horses atop the hill ahead. He put on a burst of speed, his heart filling like a sail as he left his rival behind. Belatedly he realized that they had designated no clear finish line. The top of the hill, then, Edmund decided—but as he approached, pumping harder to conquer the slope, the men shouted and brandished their spears.

"Edmund, hold!" Godfrith cried, and began shouting to the men in the Danske tunga. They put up their weapons again, but watched Edmund suspiciously as he slowed but did not stop his progress. They backed their mounts away as he topped the rise.

Grinning, he turned to offer a hand to Godfrith as he panted up the slope.

"Idiot!" said Godfrith, gulping air. "They might have killed you!" But he was half-laughing. Then he slapped Edmund on the back and called him "wolf-friend."

"I couldn't help it," said Edmund. "I always finish the race."

When he had taken leave of Godfrith, Edmund ran the whole way back to camp again for the sheer joy of running on this bright and hopeful day of redemption. The Gospel book was saved, a horse had replaced the ox, they had hopes of good relations with Danish jarls all across the land. *And!* Edmund had beat Godfrith in their race, and Godfrith had called him "wolf-friend." Land and sea spread out gloriously before his flying feet, the sunlight making jewels of light on the returning waters of the bay, and the breeze welcoming him with the mixed scent of pasture clover and salt air.

The last thing he expected to find was Hunred pounding across the field toward him, shouting his name in panic.

"What is it? What's happened?" Edmund cried in alarm as they came to a stop facing each other in the meadow. Hunred's breathing was ragged and his face knotted in torture.

"I can't—I don't know how—I—"

"Is someone hurt? Are we attacked?"

Hunred moaned and collapsed to the ground, covering his face. "No, no . . . nothing like that."

"Hunred!" Edmund scrambled down beside him and shook him by the shoulders. "*What is it?*"

Hunred took deep breaths. "We leave by the end of the week."

"Yes?" Edmund was mystified. This was not the old impassive Hunred he had known on Lindesfarne, nor the doleful penitent Hunred that had shared the cart yoke with Edmund for three years now.

"I am not to be made a novice after all."

Edmund sat back on his heels. Hunred was not looking at him, but staring off into the distance where the blue of the sky met the blue of the bay. "Hunred—you had a true vision. For years I've hated the way you gaze off into the air—"

Hunred gave him a sharp look at that, and Edmund returned him a sheepish one. "Well, all right, I was wrong, and I'm sorry about it now," Edmund said. He went on, "The point is, even I admit you had a true vision of Saint Cuthbert, and recovered the Book, and got us a horse for the cart. Why wouldn't the bishop let you be a novice now? You've done penance enough."

Hunred shook his head with a rough laugh. "He doesn't mean this as a punishment." He gazed up at the clouds above. "Just the opposite. We've received signs that things will soon be better, and we have to act in faith that we will find a home for Cuthbert. So—I'm commanded to ask Aelfleda . . . The bishop says it's time the company had a wedding again!"

Edmund blinked. "What did Stitheard say?"

"Stitheard," Hunred sighed, "said it was a splendid excuse to finish the cask of mead they opened for that visiting jarl you brought in."

Edmund snorted. "So, he's forgiven you now, or he wouldn't tease you like that."

"But Edmund, what if she says no? She's hardly spoken to me since the day we went to sea at Derwentmouth! And since then I've watched her all the time, hoping maybe she might thaw, but she always turns away when she sees me. And I always think, well, maybe that's better, since I'm going to be a novice anyway. But now I'm not, and the bishop insists I must *ask* her!"

Edmund shook his head, suppressing a laugh. "Hunred, you're just lucky this is Aelfleda we're talking about. If it were Caris, she would probably have smacked your face the first time she caught you looking at her!"

Hunred frowned, plucked a sun-centered day's eye flower and began to remove the petals one by one, muttering, "Yes, no, maybe so . . ." Then he threw it down. "Caris doesn't smack *your* face when you look at her," he said accusingly. "Why don't *you* ask *her*, and you can be the one having a wedding tomorrow?"

"Because the bishop didn't order *me* to ask a girl to marry me," Edmund said smugly.

Hunred sighed. "Do you think you could ask her *for* me?"

"Hunred!"

"Well—could you ask *Caris* to ask her if she would say yes or no, then?"

Edmund got to his feet, rolling his eyes. "Hunred! Just tell her you're sorry about taking back your promise before, and all you want in the world is for her to say *Yes!* Go do it and get it over with!"

Then he marched away shaking his head, before Hunred could say any more.

chapter twenty-four

THE WEDDING WAS CELEBRATED BEFORE THE RELICS of Saint Cuthbert the next morning, and two days later the haliwerfolc packed up and headed off, spirits soaring higher than they had ever done in the company's long pilgrimage. Only one thing disappointed Edmund: The day the Gospel book was found, Riddle disappeared and did not return.

That summer brought the best harvest in years, and that in turn brought the company a kinder welcome at many stopping places than they had known in a long time. They traveled less urgently, and found that Godfrith's name opened doors to them on the lands in his list, which were occupied by Danes friendly to him. "Guthfrith" his name was pronounced in their speech … but many of them now were learning the English tongue too, which the bishop remarked was a promising sign. Danes and Angles alike were not too grudging of hospitality after the good harvest, but all talked much of the uncertain future and lack of a clear leader among the remnants of the great host that still occupied Eoforwic.

"We'd best learn to call it 'Jorvik' like they do," the bishop had told them.

"These are all 'if' promises," Edmund said to Hunred one snowy day in Christmastide as they stabled Sigr after a morning's exercise, at yet another estate where they had stayed two weeks now, in the moors east of the Pennines. The company called them moors—the Danes who now held this isolated estate called them fells. But they had agreed to pay a stonesmith to set up a carved cross on their lands, and promised a church one day—*if*, as Edmund had just pointed out, all went well.

"I gave an 'if' promise once," said Hunred as they curried the horse's coat. "It turned out better than expected."

It had not been that hard for Edmund and the rest of the saint-bearers to get used to the new, mellow Hunred, who being married now was excused from the roster for night watch. No one grudged it to him, as he went about his daytime chores with a dreamy good humor.

Even Franco had dropped one or two remarks about perhaps giving up his long novitiate. Edmund watched him closely, because he suspected the cause of those thoughts was none other than Edmund's own little sister Merewyn. Not so little any more, she wore the woman's veil over her pale hair now, and turned heads wherever the company went.

Aelfleda still told stories, which won the Danes' women and children and intrigued the men. But these days, Hunred stood beside her the whole time, frowning at any man who seemed more interested in looking than listening.

Once Aelfleda had softened them up, the bishop went on to preach and baptize many of these people. They would come to Cuthbert's relics for prayer and healing, and many of the prayers were answered swiftly and visibly.

"Waes hal, Mother!" Hunred called, looking over Edmund's shoulder.

"There you both are!" she said with satisfaction.

Edmund glanced back at the open barn door. While Hunred secured the horse in his stall and brought him a forkful of hay, Edmund murmured under his breath, "What have we done now?"

"Good day, Mother," he said aloud, as she kissed him on both cheeks, then went on to do the same with Hunred.

"Well. There you both are," she said again, as she stood back and admired them. Edmund and Hunred looked at each other.

"It's you I've come for, mind you, Edmund," she said, frowning a little.

"Me! What did I do?"

"It's what you haven't done, my boy. I've a mind to see some grandchildren before I go blind with age."

"Mother! Are you going blind?" Hunred asked, suddenly panicked.

She sighed in exasperation. "No, Hunred. And I wasn't speaking to you."

"Why not?" said Edmund. "He's the one that's married!"

"Well! *Now* you are beginning to understand!" she said, poking him in the chest with one of her age-spotted hands. "Just *what* is keeping you, Edmund?"

"I—well, nothing, I just—well, I'm just finishing the race, that's all!"

She stood staring at him, arms folded. Then she said, "Hmmph!" shook her head, and tramped away out of the barn again.

Hunred fetched a bucket of water for Sigr's trough, avoiding meeting Edmund's eyes. Edmund cast around for something else to do, but there was nothing. As he was about to head out the stable door, Stitheard came in.

"That's it," he said. "We're off again in two days—and listen, boys, there's real news this time!"

"What is it?" said Edmund.

Stitheard grinned at them, relishing his chance to make the announcement. "There's a place called Crec, which land belonged to Lindesfarne before all the trouble started—before even the Danes, during all the infighting by rival kings of our own Northumbria before that. It's not far from Eoforwic—Jorvik as the Danes call it now—and it's been let be for some time now. There are monks there, with a little timber church, and they are ready for us to come and stay there as long as we like!"

"Thanks be to God!" said Hunred. "Oh, Aelfleda will be so glad! She didn't want to tell anyone yet, but—" He stopped and looked at the other two, who stared, mouths open.

Hunred looked like he was going to burst. Stitheard whooped and took him in a bear hug while Hunred nodded, eyes round and a kind of terrified grin on his face.

Edmund slapped him on the back. "*What* did Mother just say? You go tell her this minute!"

"And then we'll need a drink, son!" said Stitheard, and dragged Hunred off out of the barn. Edmund was relieved to be left behind. Maybe this news would keep his mother's attention off *him* for a bit!

<hr />

AS IT HAPPENED, THEY VISITED MANY MORE ESTATES, AND only finally came late in summer to Crec, where they found all as promised. The abbot was named Geve, and he had persuaded the local jarl, who had become a Christian when he married a Northumbrian woman, to return the land to the Church. Geve and the bishop and Abbot Eadred spent much time with heads together, and visiting the local jarl and other Danish lords who came up to Crec from Eoforwic. Meanwhile, the layfolk and monks were busy building themselves shelter for the winter. Even the saint-bearers took a share in this, using Sigr to draw felled trees to the building site, while the holy coffin rested in the little timber church belonging to the monks of Crec.

Edmund was glad of the work, but as the days lengthened a certain melancholy came over him. It looked like they might be here permanently . . .

One afternoon, Edmund borrowed a hook and line, the tools of inland fishing. After a fruitless hour crouched on the bank he heard, "Why so glum, Edmund son of Tida?" Abbot Eadred sat down beside him. Hair more wool-white than gray now, he still looked hale as ever.

"I don't even know," Edmund admitted.

"I am on my way to see the bishop. I have had a new dream. Peace is coming to Dane and Angle alike in Northumbria, and the haliwerfolc will have a new home for their saint."

Edmund's heart leapt, and suddenly he knew why the waning year sat so heavily upon him: The pilgrimage was nearly over, and he wanted to go home. He wanted salt air and the old hut on the beach, the cry of the gulls and the sound of Lindesfarne's church bell. "Lindesfarne?"

"Hmm. Well, I don't know where. But here is the news, Edmund—Saint Cuthbert tells me there will be a new king for Angles and Danes both, and it should be your friend Godfrith."

"Godfrith!" Maybe it shouldn't have been so surprising—but Edmund found the idea that he was personally acquainted with a king too strange for words.

"Yes. Your friend Godfrith was born a Dane, but fostered by Angles. I am leaving for Whittingham tomorrow to fetch him. And you, Edmund, will come with me. You will ride Sigr. Go and pack up now!"

Thrill and apprehension rose in him. "But I've never really learned to ride!" Edmund objected.

"I will teach you as we go. Besides," he grinned as he headed off again, "Saint Cuthbert will help you. He gave us that horse, didn't he?"

Edmund hastily wound up his fishing line on the spool, setting the hook carefully into the twine. He made his way up the bank and started running across the field, where barley had been lately harvested. Here and there women and children were gleaning fallen stalks of grain. To the left, he could see Abbot Eadred crossing the field and veering off in the direction of the church. Edmund continued straight across the field toward the stable.

Riding with Eadred! And going to see Godfrith again—and Godfrith to be king! Edmund's feet pounded joyfully along between the rows of stubble, and when he spotted Caris ahead, even her folded arms and frown did not dampen his mood.

"Did the abbot tell you?" Edmund said eagerly as he ground to a halt before her.

"He said you wanted to see me."

"What? No, I never said—"

"He said you would say that. And he said if you didn't want to see me, you *ought* to want to see me, and you ought to want it right now."

Edmund was taken aback. "What? Why?"

"Because, Edmund son of Tida, I have not one but two offers to wed. One in the company, one among the Danes at Crec Hall. That one doesn't speak English, but he's the handsomest man on the estate, and he owns five acres of land."

"What!" Edmund dropped the spool of fishing line and forgot about the horse. "You can't marry a Dane! You didn't leave the company for your own brother, and your own estates at Aelfsdene. Why would you leave now for a Dane?"

"I'm not *leaving*, Edmund. The company is at home now."

"No, we aren't! Eadred just told me—he isn't sure where we'll be. It might be Lindesfarne, it might be here, it might be somewhere else entirely."

"Oh." It was Caris's turn to be set on her heels. "Well. All right, then. Never mind the Dane. Though he *is* good-looking, and landed as well. But I still have another in the company— and I *will* choose him, Edmund son of Tida, unless you speak up quick!"

When Edmund was struck dumb by this, she hastily put on a manner more haughty than any he had seen her use since Doddington Moor. "What I mean is, if you want to be in that race, I will consider your name too."

Edmund's jaw dropped. "There is not one man in this company better than me—that is, if I *wanted* to be in that race."

"Well, you are late off the mark already. Franco asked me this morning," she said, smug as a cat. "The moment Bishop Eardwulf released him from the novitiate."

"Franco!" cried Edmund. What an outrageous thought! "I don't believe you—he's always hanging about with Merewyn."

Caris stooped to pick up the half-filled gleaning basket at her feet. "Edmund, you dunce. He only hangs about Merewyn when she happens to be with me. Merewyn's always fancied Cuthwin."

"Cuthwin?" This was getting crazier all the time. "Cuthwin's a child! So is Merewyn, come to that."

Caris looked at him and shrugged. "Children grow up. But I've been of age a good long while now and I'm not waiting any longer." She turned to head back toward the camp near the half-finished building site west of the field, but Edmund grabbed her by the arms and spun her back about to face him.

"I said I wouldn't promise," he said through clenched teeth, "because I have to finish my race—to bear the saint to a new home. I told you all that at Workington, just to be honest with you. But look at you now—leading on a novice and flirting with some Dane, when all the while you know very well it's only me you want!"

Caris gasped in indignation, but Edmund quickly slid his hands down her arms to grasp her wrists so she couldn't slap him. She set her jaw while he grinned in triumph.

"All right then," she said, glowering at him. "You just see if I am bluffing, Edmund son of Tida. You just *dare* not to admit you want me too, and I will say yes to that Dane today. Today!"

They stood toe-to-toe, Edmund still clenching her wrists in his hands. "Well . . . you *are* the fairest maiden in all the company," he said grudgingly.

Her eyes narrowed. "Don't you bother trying to flatter me. You're no good at it."

He let her go. "And you're too clever for it," he admitted.

"So the only question," Caris said, "is who is the most stubborn."

"Oh, there's no question," said Edmund, a slow grin spreading on his face. "It's you. That's why, after Godfrith is made king, I'm going to marry you."

He grabbed her arms again, kissed her quick, then scooped up his fishing spool and ran like the wind, laughing all the way to the stable.

chapter twenty-five

IT WAS A TOUR OF SEVERAL WEEKS WITH EADRED AND a party of monks, thegns, and jarls who were friendly to Godfrith, up along the old Roman road called Dere Street. It stretched away north, broad and busy, and Edmund frankly gawked at the numerous companies of English folk and Danes they met that were heading south to Jorvik with market goods: harvest surplus, wool, cloth, and more. The traffic slowed their progress, for they stopped to exchange news with them all.

Edmund found it exhilarating, but for one thing: despite Abbot Eadred's optimism, Sigr had proven feisty and mischievous, dumping the inexperienced Edmund from his back at the worst times—usually in the mud. The others in the party laughed, but Eadred would not allow Edmund to exchange mounts with anyone.

"He is Saint Cuthbert's horse, and you are the only saintbearer in our party," the abbot said.

Before they crossed the Tyne, the party began breaking into

smaller groups, heading in various directions to persuade others to their cause. It had been agreed, there would be a king chosen at Michaelmas upon Oswiesdune near Crec, before the holy relics of Saint Cuthbert.

Edmund continued with Abbot Eadred and some others up the Rede Valley to Osbert's lands. They found the thegn of Aelfsdene in high spirits, his bride of a year having just given him a son. Osbert was glad to hear that the pin had been passed on to Caris, and that she was well. To Edmund's amusement, he seemed to have forgotten Aelfleda entirely.

As they sat at table that night, Osbert asked, "What's become of your raven, Edmund?"

Edmund shook his head sadly. "He was never really mine. He comes and goes. The last time I saw him was in the spring, near Hwitern."

The next day, Osbert rode with them to Whittingham. As they made their way in fine crisp weather through the autumn-clad hills, the talk of course turned on Godfrith, who had the support of all the Northumbrian thegns north of the Tyne. The smaller number of scattered Danes who had settled in this north country were somewhat less certain of him, but even they had no other preferred candidates.

"Tell Osbert how you helped Godfrith kill the wolves, Edmund," said Abbot Eadred. He had a mischievous glint in his eye.

He knows this embarrasses me, thought Edmund. But there was nothing for it but to tell the tale.

When it was done, Osbert said, "He never told me about that. But then, that's how Godfrith is. Close. I've known him since we were boys—his foster father Wistan, the thegn of Whittingham, was friends with my father. To tell you the truth, Edmund,

I've always been afraid Godfrith and I would end up on opposite sides of a battle some day."

Abbot Eadred said, "God willing, soon there won't be any sides."

The autumn sun slanted down behind them when they trotted up to the gate of Whittingham's yard. A young guard welcomed them, but no sooner were the men and horses through than a strange-looking old woman wandered out toward them, muttering to herself. As she came closer, Edmund saw that for some reason she had stuck chicken feathers all around her head in the ribbon that bound on her veil. Her face was wrinkled and her feet were bare, and when she saw the men and horses she suddenly let out a wail and complained about being robbed.

It was so disconcerting Edmund didn't even notice where Godfrith came from when he appeared at the woman's side and kindly took her by the arm. "Come, Tola, there is soup waiting for you in the hall."

But Tola wagged her finger at Abbot Eadred and cried, "*You!* You stole my slave. You must pay!"

"Tola, this is Abbot Eadred. He did not steal any slave."

"Well then, he owes me the price for the one he bought!"

Godfrith looked up at the abbot apologetically, then leaned toward him and said in a low voice, "It's better if you just give her a small coin."

Eadred smiled and nodded. The party dismounting, he bade his purser give the Lady Tola a copper penig.

She took it and smiled, then turned away to walk toward the hall, but before Godfrith could get on with his greeting of the visitors, she cried out and whirled around again. "Godfrith! Oh, Godfrith, I've sold you!" And she began to weep.

Once again Godfrith consoled her. "It's all right, Tola," he said, an arm about her shaking old shoulders. "Listen," he whispered loudly into ears that must have been a little deaf, "I will go with the new master, and escape like I did before. I'll come back soon. All right?"

After a little more persuasion, the old lady of Whittingham went on back toward the hall, where her women took her in.

Godfrith apologized to his guests and called the stable boys to care for their mounts. While the travelers drank and washed at the well, he said to Edmund, "Tola was good to me when I was a boy and a stranger here. When I escaped Thorstein at Shotton and came back here, I told her how he and his men had treated me like a slave. Now she's a little wandering in her mind and sometimes thinks I'm a slave. She's afraid I'll be taken away again."

Edmund understood why men were ready to follow Godfrith. Killing Thorstein had perhaps impressed some, but there was something stronger still in his grateful kindness to his gently mad old foster mother.

Next morning, they set out anew, this time with Godfrith and some of his men. Over the course of several days, they stopped at a string of estates and towns, coming at last to what had been the Northumbrian royal fort of Bebbanbyrig on the coast.

"I remember visiting here with Bishop Eardwulf when I was first a messenger boy," said Edmund as they trotted up to the imposing timber gate at sunset. "I didn't really understand what was happening in those days, or why King Ricsige didn't defend us against the Danes. But I could tell the bishop didn't like him."

"Because he was nothing but a playing piece on Halfdan's gameboard," said Abbot Eadred, shaking his head sadly. "He let the invaders take what they liked from his people, and Bishop Eardwulf could not make him promise to see Lindesfarne safe. That was why we had to take Cuthbert and go."

But Ricsige was years dead now, and the thegn in charge of Bebbanbyrig supported Godfrith, greeting him as if he were already king. He showed the abbot deference too, as did a large number of both Angles and Danes gathered there.

Edmund found the political talk dull, and all his mind bent on one desire that had been growing in him since they left Whittingham: Lindesfarne would actually be in sight across the water from Bebbanbyrig when the sun rose, and Edmund meant to see it. So next morning in the cold dawn light, he slipped out of the hall and called up to the man in the tall timber guard tower.

The man was not co-operative. "But I'm the saint-bearer," Edmund begged. "I was born on Lindesfarne, and haven't seen it for more than six years now. Please!"

"Guard!" came a voice from behind Edmund, and he turned to find Godfrith there. "Come down and let us up!"

The man scrambled down, apologizing repeatedly till it made Godfrith laugh and tell him he had done well to obey the rules. He climbed up the ladder with Edmund behind him, coming out onto the platform hedged about with a wooden rail. Edmund strained eagerly toward the northeast, but the morning mist hid the island.

"There's no place like it," he sighed.

"I've never crossed," said Godfrith, "But tomorrow I make a pilgrimage there. Last night I made my first confession since my baptism as a boy, and the abbot told me I must go to the Holy Island and pray before we set out for the south. Truthfully, Edmund," he lowered his voice because of the guard still waiting at the foot of the tower, "I grow a bit weary of the constant attendance of so many. What say you and I slip out together on our horses before dawn tomorrow, and make for Lindesfarne?"

"Oh, yes," Edmund said eagerly. "But we should have to wait on the tide to cross with horses. Why not a boat?"

So a boat it was, next day. The tide was running high when they set out, and though he could see his own old home as they approached, Edmund decided to pass by the harbor and land Godfrith on the tiny islet called Saint Cuthbert's Isle. It was only a few rods long and wide, and bare of anything but stone and grass. Only a stone's throw away were the monastery grounds on Lindesfarne itself.

"Cuthbert used to come here to pray at times alone, but it was still too close to the monastery, so that's why he went off to make his hermitage on Farne," Edmund explained.

"Sad to see this chapel in ruins," said Godfrith, for the stones had tumbled in on each other.

Edmund sighed deeply, for he had been told by the Bebban-byrig folk that the church and monastery buildings had been burnt by Halfdan's men, and Edmund and Godfrith had seen the blackened beams of the skeletal church roof from the water. "Godfrith—if you are king, will you give Lindesfarne back to the Church?"

"I will, Edmund. But Bishop Eardwulf and I have already discussed a new home for the saint—partway between here and Jorvik, at the old Roman fort in Cuncaceastre."

Edmund's heart had risen suddenly, and now it was dashed again. "What? Why? No! You can't! We've wandered years—we want to come home!" Dismay flooded him. "The bishop meant to take our saint to Ireland—that was wrong, and so is this."

After a moment Godfrith said evenly, "You know, Edmund, Abbot Eadred told me that Saint Cuthbert was first made prior of Lindesfarne to reconcile the monks of the Irish and Roman parties in the Church of his day. I think that to have the saint today in the midst of the kingdom, instead of on this distant island, may bring peace to Danes and Angles and all."

A whirlpool of feelings thrashed about inside Edmund. To be so close to home, here at Lindesfarne, and learn it was not to be . . . and maybe worst of all, being strangely reminded just now of Derwin by Godfrith's calm, reasonable words. Edmund turned away, ashamed to show his tears of anger and frustration. "You came here to pray, you said. Well, the tide is ebbing again now, you can walk across the sands to the monastery grounds before long. I'll meet you at the church about noon."

Godfrith called his thanks, but Edmund, his throat tight with anger and disappointment, said no more as he launched the little boat and began to row around the point to the harbor. He beached the craft, strode up the shore to his old house, and went in to look at the sad remains: roof straw beaten by storms into a net, straw beds and rushes on the floor rotted black. He went out again and began to run, up along the path inland that he had taken that day seven years ago when the bell summoned the haliwerfolc to the end of their island life.

Topping the rise, he turned not left to the monastery, but right along the cartway toward the hall. He ran, not fast and desperate as he had when the bishop sent him out as a boy to test him that first time, nor wild and fearful as on that day when they were told the monks must leave Lindesfarne. He ran steadily, numbly, as if in a dream that refused to end. Past fields gone to seed and pastures engulfed by thistles. He saw the blackened ruins of the hall ahead, stared at them a moment when he reached the yard that had once teemed with activity, and turned right again to head for Beblow Crag, the high lookout point on the southeast corner of the island. He climbed the Crag, stood and looked about in all directions. It was not yet noon. White clouds loomed from the mainland, their bottoms flat and unthreatening as they sailed toward the island, while the blue of the sky remained undaunted. No sails dotted the easy swells of the sea, and to the south Edmund could see clear to the fort at Bebbanbyrig, which made a dark lump on the horizon before him, with the flatter splotches of the Farne Islands to its left. *Holy men and kings . . .* what was to become of ordinary people like fishermen's sons in this new Northumbria?

Though his heart was sore with homesickness, he knew better than to linger in self-pity for long. He came down from the Crag and set out along the beach, running fast now because he could. The tide had gone out, leaving the smell of seaweed, and gulls squabbling about the tidepools. He came full circle back to the little boat in front of his old home.

The sun stood nearly overhead now, but Edmund found himself reluctant still to join Godfrith at the ruined monastery church. Up the bank and across the island he jogged again. *Saying goodbye to Lindesfarne with my feet,* he thought. He went on past the burnt-out guest house by the burnt-down gate, and along to the western shore, where the sands now stretched to the mainland. The water would soon begin to come in to cover them again. They were bare and lonely; Edmund knew Bishop Eardwulf had given orders the first day to the people at Beehall to come and remove the wooden crosses that marked the pilgrim way, to make it harder for any Danes to cross. But it seemed not to have stopped them, and now the monastery was a charred ruin.

Bare and lonely? Distant figures moved on the shore. No, not on the shore—on the sands, coming toward the island. Edmund stared. Mounted figures, five of them, coming quickly across the sands. It shouldn't be anyone from Bebbanbyrig; he knew Godfrith had told Eadred his plans to come by boat with Edmund alone.

And whoever they are, they've seen me standing exposed on this shore now too.

Edmund turned and ran for the church.

"GODFRITH!" EDMUND CRIED AS HE SKIDDED TO A HALT IN the yard. All around him lay the blackened timbers of what used to be the familiar monastery buildings—the church, the refectory, the school hall. "Godfrith!"

He ought to be here by now. Edmund scrambled through the ruins and made his way up onto the Heugh, the ridge that looked out on the sea to the south of the monastery grounds. From its western end Edmund could see that there was no one on Saint Cuthbert's Isle. He ran to the other end of the Heugh, out along the eastern promontory that let him overlook the harbor. There far up the beach he saw a tiny figure that had to be Godfrith. But when he tried to call, the wind and waves took his words. *So it's a race again,* thought Edmund. *All right.* And off he went, passing the beached boat and his old hut. Godfrith had almost reached Beblow Crag when Edmund had caught up enough to make himself heard, so that Godfrith turned and came toward him. Only then did Edmund notice the black bird that perched on Godfrith's shoulder, when it flapped off and circled Godfrith's head.

"Edmund, look! I've found your raven—or he found me."

Edmund found himself out of breath—not from running, but from fear and confusion.

"Cronk! Cronk!" cried the raven.

Was it really Riddle—had he found his way all the way home to Lindesfarne? But there was no time right now—"Godfrith, there are five horsemen coming across the sands!"

Godfrith frowned. "A message shouldn't need so many bearers . . . Well, but I haven't been to the church yet—the bird led me off the isle, Edmund! And then up the beach . . . so I just kept following."

"Godfrith. Are you sure all those jarls and thegns that were at Bebbanbyrig last night are on your side?"

Godfrith laughed. "Oh, Edmund, of course I'm not sure. We won't be sure till we get to Oswiesdune."

"How can you laugh?" Edmund was appalled. "We should leave."

"But what if they're bringing some urgent message after all?"

"Well, then, let *me* go see. If it's safe I'll let you know."

Riddle continued to circle above.

"So, the king-elect is going to skulk around on the beach and let one of the saint's holy bearers go and face his enemies for him?" Godfrith said reproachfully. "That wouldn't win me the respect of all those warlike jarls at Jorvik and Tyne."

Why did Godfrith have to pick a time like this to be stubborn? "At least help me drag the boat nearer the water so we can launch quickly if we need to."

"Oh, very well."

They jogged back down the beach, Edmund turning in frustration every few steps while Godfrith, less sure of himself than Edmund on the mixed sand and pebble surface, picked his way. "Come on! Race me!"

"Ha!" Godfrith took up the challenge with a grin. Edmund still pulled well ahead of him, eyes on the beached boat. He had just begun to feel a little less anxious when a cry of pain came from Godfrith.

"I've turned an ankle on these cursed slippery stones!"

chapter twenty-six

D READ SETTLED INTO EDMUND'S CHEST. HE WENT back to steady Godfrith as he limped the rest of the way to the boat at the far end of the beach. There the two of them dragged the little craft laboriously across the sands toward the waves while Riddle perched on the prow, criticizing their every move.

The flock of fleecy clouds that had passed overhead from the west that morning now joined up with a black-looking mass over the sea to the northeast. And the wind was changing. Edmund called a halt a few rods from the surf, eying it doubtfully.

"Out anchor now and let the incoming tide float the boat?" asked Godfrith. He made no complaint about his ankle, but Edmund could see the pain in his face.

"Yes," said Edmund, and lifted out the heavy anchor rock on its tether of thick rope. "But . . . if we aren't ready to go in time, we'll have to wade through surf or swim, and it's deadly cold for that."

A shout from the shore. Godfrith turned. "Too late."

Edmund sprang to plant himself in front of Godfrith. The men had dismounted and now strode purposefully but without hurry across the sand toward them. The hair on the back of Edmund's neck rose at the sight of the coppery hair and beard of the leader. "*Miserere nobis!* It's Frana!" Frana son of Thorstein, who had a blood grudge against Godfrith.

Godfrith stepped forward, drawing his blade. "Keep back, Edmund. I have to face him sooner or later."

Hunred was right, Edmund thought, *all those years ago when he broke my little driftwood sword . . . Those who live by the sword shall perish by the sword.*

"Frana!" called Godfrith. "My man is unarmed, and you outnumber us. What do you come for—murder, or an honorable fight before witnesses such as your father gave me?"

Frana and his men continued to walk toward him, but they grinned, and their stride turned to a swagger. They did not draw their swords—yet. They halted a few rods distant, the armsmen spread out behind and to each side of their jarl. Indignation rose up in Edmund when he realized that at least two of the men now with Frana had been at Bebbanbyrig talking support for Godfrith last night. *Spies and traitors!* he thought.

"I will have witnesses, Hardacnut's son." Frana grinned, and looked at Edmund with contempt. "But not this churl. Fight me before all the jarls when they gather at Oswiesdune, and let the winner be king!"

"You're mad!" Edmund burst out. "People want Godfrith— they won't accept you even if you win!"

"Edmund!" Godfrith said sharply, while Frana's eyes turned to knives of hatred, twisting fear in Edmund's heart. Godfrith said, "I will fight you, Frana, but not at Oswiesdune. We will fight before those now gathered at Bebbanbyrig, tonight or tomorrow."

"No," said Frana. "I have the grievance, my father's blood on your sword, and I choose the place and time."

Edmund's heart jumped into his throat as Godfrith lifted his sword. "Choose other than Oswiesdune, Frana, or I choose this moment, witnesses or no. Refuse and I call you coward."

Edmund leapt forward. "I can beat any of your men in a foot race!"

"Call your dog to heel, Guthfrith!" Frana snarled.

"Pick one of them!" said Edmund. "The winner gets to choose the time and place for you to fight!"

Frana eyed them both suspiciously for a moment, his hand on his sword hilt. Then he turned to one of his men, a lanky-limbed fellow with a prominent forehead and frizzy beard, calling him "Svein" and exchanging a few words in Danske. Then he nodded at Godfrith, who sheathed his sword.

They all went up the bank and inland to the cartway. Edmund thought it must be costing Godfrith some pain not to show his limp to his enemies. Frana sent one of his horsemen along the path a few furlongs, where he dismounted and laid his sword carefully across the path. Edmund guffawed in disbelief. "That's a girl's race! I want a race to the other end of the island. And back. Or is that too much for your man, Jarl Frana?"

That wiped the smiles from their faces. But after a moment, Frana growled and agreed. The man who had laid down his sword was sent to gallop to the other end of the island and place it there as the center point of the race.

"I have no other man to go and watch at the center point. Do you swear by Odin to run a fair race?" Godfrith asked Frana.

"By Odin and Thor!" said the jarl, drawing out his little hammer pendant and holding it up. Then he laid his own sword down on the ground for the finish line.

"Cronk! Cronk!" Riddle called above them, and swooped down to land on Godfrith's shoulder. Frana's men started backward, cursing in Danske, but Frana himself stared at the bird, and then at Edmund. Edmund swallowed. *He recognizes me now, and he knows that I was involved in Godfrith's escape from Shotton.*

His rival Svein was visibly shaken by the bird, but when they stood together at the start line Edmund realized just how long-legged the man was. *Cuthbert help me!* he thought, and crossed himself.

"Ein! Tveir! Thrir!"

Like arrows they sped down the cartway. Edmund's feet knew it all from of old. He only had to keep them from running away with him, for Svein was an untried opponent, and Edmund kept pace with him, saving his strength for the way back.

They got as far as the departure point for the pilgrim way when the rain started coming down. Neither of them heeded it. Edmund set his sights on the blackened hulk of the hall, in front of which as agreed the horseman waited behind the line to watch the racers leap over the blade and turn around. As they closed on the mark, Edmund dropped back and let Svein go ahead. There was plenty of time to catch him on the way back.

But just before reaching the blade, Svein skidded in the mud and lost his balance. *Oh, well!* thought Edmund, and leapt merrily past him and across the sword. He waved cockily at the grimacing horseman, then turned around and sped back across the sword and away down the road while Svein was still struggling to his feet.

Not too fast, and don't look back, Edmund reminded himself. But a moment later he was startled to find the horse galloping up beside him, the rider once more holding his sword high. He did not use it against Edmund, but turned his mount across Edmund's path, and to avoid colliding with the animal's flank he had to change course quickly. *Dirty trick!* he thought, and the fury made him run faster.

A moment later Frana's man did it again. Although Edmund was prepared this time, he landed in a boggy spot, and before he could extract himself, Svein pounded past at a speed that told Edmund he too had been saving his strength. Edmund's shoe came away in the sucking mud, and he threw the other one after it and went on. The bone-chilling rain hammered at him, the road tore at his soles, and his breath came in gasps. At least the horseman had gone on to the finish line now. Edmund gained on Svein—but not fast enough.

Please, Cuthbert, for Northumbria, for Godfrith, for all the company of the haliwerfolc, pray God to help me!

Through the obscuring curtain of the rain he could see the growing figure of his rival, and beyond him a furlong or so the others waiting at the finish line. *Now, O angels of God, now please!* thought Edmund, and made ready to burst his heart with the last leg.

Somewhere in the gale he thought he could hear Riddle calling furiously. Then the wind gusted violently from the east at his back, and he nearly felt it was sweeping him forward off his feet. Svein looked back, astonished to see him there, and Edmund sailed on past him, leaping across Frana's sword with a triumphant shout of "God and Saint Cuthbert!"

Svein, panting, crossed the sword several strides behind him.

"Tomorrow at Bebbanbyrig, Frana!" said Godfrith.

Frana picked up his sword without speaking, and he and all his men mounted their horses and turned for the mainland. Edmund swayed dizzily against Godfrith.

"We're a fine pair," said Godfrith. "Let's see if we can find any shelter in one of the harbor huts."

But something was tugging at Edmund's thoughts, and he stood there like a man with a fishing net, then suddenly hauled the thing aboard. "Godfrith—the tide! They don't know the Pilgrim Way, and the markers are gone!"

So Edmund ran yet again, calling ahead to the horsemen, who did not look back. He remembered Herebert and Frisk racing the tide that calm bright day seven years ago, and knowing the monk would make it, barely, because rider and horse were guided by the crosses that used to stand there. Now Edmund ran, feet bloody, gasping for breath and shaking from the chilling rain, ran like a madman after mounted enemies to save their lives.

The horsemen were already on the sands, though less than halfway across, when Edmund reached the shore. The rain was easing but the wind blew stronger than ever, and the tidewaters were rushing in from both ends of the island, beginning to pool amongst the shifting sands and small stones of the crossing. Edmund cupped his hands about his mouth for a desperate halloo, and against all hope he saw one of the now distant figures turn toward him. He waved his hands frantically and called, "Frana!"

Frana gestured at his men to go on, and trotted back toward Lindesfarne. Edmund ran toward him, shouting, "Tell them to come back!"

But Frana kept coming, drawing his sword as he dug his heels into his horse to speed it toward Edmund.

Edmund stopped. *I'm dead*, he thought. *But I was trying to save his life!*

He made the sign of the cross and stood still while the Dane thundered toward him. But he did not fall to his knees, lest Frana think he was begging for mercy.

The horse galloped by, and Frana, laughing wildly, whirled his sword around, the blade cutting through the air just inches above Edmund's head. He circled Edmund, twirling the sword. "You like to run, English dog? Run! Run for your life!" He made another taunting pass of the blade over Edmund's head.

The race is over, Edmund thought but didn't say aloud. And didn't run, and didn't move.

The tide's long arms were reaching around both ends of Lindesfarne for a watery embrace, but the waves did not yet meet. Frana's men might make it. But if Frana headed back now, his chances of crossing were poor indeed.

I should just let him drown. He's going to kill me anyway. Why should Godfrith have to fight him tomorrow with that hurt ankle?

For a moment it seemed a possible choice. But then he shouted at Frana, "I came to warn you! The sands shift, and the currents are treacherous. You won't make it!"

"Frana!" Godfrith hailed from the shore, hurrying toward them with his limp now quite apparent. Riddle left his shoulder and flew out toward them, cawing belligerently.

Godfrith's sword rang out. "Let my man be, Frana! He isn't a warrior."

Frana grinned. "But perhaps his blood on my sword would make tomorrow's fight sweeter, Guthfrith!"

But with Frana's attention distracted, Edmund dashed away to the side. Riddle cheered him. Now Godfrith's sword was between him and their enemy.

"Will you get off that horse and fight me now, Frana?"

For answer the jarl jumped off his horse and swung his blade downward at Godfrith. Godfrith met the stroke with his own sword, and they went at it. Edmund's heart was in his mouth as he watched them exchange clashing blows. Before long he saw Godfrith favoring the injured foot. Then Frana saw it too, and lunged eagerly forward. But he was taken by surprise, for the fight ended suddenly and not in his favor after all. Godfrith stepped forward to meet him, not with a stroke to any vital spot, but up against his sword hand, cutting deep at the wrist. With a howl Frana's arm jerked, and the sword went sailing across the shore.

Edmund ran to retrieve it. He brought it and stood with it before him, point down in the sand, a few paces behind and beside Godfrith.

"We are both injured," said Godfrith to Frana. "Call truce now and let us meet another day."

"Another day? You've beaten him!" Edmund exclaimed. "This was the fight he wanted, and you won, Godfrith! He should just go home and give it up now."

Frana glared at them, nursing his bleeding hand. "A blood feud does not go home, English dog. I will never give it up." He clambered into the saddle one-handed and goaded the horse across the sands.

"No!" cried Edmund. "Frana! Come back, you can't make it!"

But Frana did not look back. He raced his horse for the mainland while the tide came on, relentlessly cutting off the path both before and behind, the currents boiling up, more violent than Edmund had ever seen them. Frana and his horse were small distant figures when the water took them, but Edmund still had to turn his eyes away while he made the sign of the cross.

AFTER A COMFORTLESS NIGHT IN A HALF-RUINED HUT, AT THE morning ebb the weather cleared and they were able to get back to the boat. When they had raised the sail and were underway with Riddle circling the mast, Godfrith sat staring at Frana's sword where it lay in the bottom of the boat.

"Edmund, I just realized," he said, "when you came to Whittingham, I entirely forgot to give you back your friend's sword!"

Edmund was silent a moment while he adjusted the tiller. Then he said, "I don't think I want it after all. Seems I'm a runner, not a swordsman."

"Edmund—don't accuse me of trying to buy friendship again, but what reward can I give you for winning that very important race?"

Edmund looked down at his feet, then up at Godfrith with a smile. "A new pair of shoes?"

epilogue

ON THE EVE OF MICHAELMAS, THE LORDS AND MANY
common folk from all over Northumbria who camped
about Oswiesdune numbered in the thousands. The
lords confirmed the election of Godfrith, with only a few com-
plainers offering the most token objection.

Michaelmas itself dawned clear and cold, and Edmund was
glad of the new-woven cloak Godfrith had given each of the
bearers, so that monk and layman alike might attend Cuthbert's
cart as a matched band in finery fit for the occasion. Lady Tola
might be mad, but she and her women had woven a black-and-
white checked cloth of stunning quality. All of the bearers had
new tunics or habits of undyed wool as well, and the cloaks fastened at the shoulder with bronze cross-shaped pins presented
by Osbert. Even Sigr wore silver bells and harness trappings
to pull the coffin cart, which was fitted now with carved and
painted decorations.

As the procession passed the assembled haliwerfolc on its way
up the hill, Caris's admiring gaze warmed Edmund from the

inside, even better than the cloak warmed against the November air from without. She too wore a new gown and cloak, a gift Edmund had delivered to her from Osbert's wife, her new sister-in-law, and the flashing gold enamel pin that had been her mother's made her the best-dressed woman there. But her eyes were the real jewels . . .

"Lords of Northumbria!" cried the bishop from the hilltop. "Will you have Guthfrith, son of Hardacnut, to be king over you, Yea or Nay?"

Swords rang from sheaths, and the assembled leaders raised them flashing in the morning sunlight with a mighty roar of "Yea!"

The saint-bearers stood ranged to either side of the coffin, so Edmund could see the whole ceremony at close range. Godfrith in a garnet-red cloak and madder-blue tunic knelt before Cuthbert's relics, and Abbot Eadred held out the great jewel-covered Gospel book for him to kiss. With a Latin pronouncement Bishop Eardwulf poured the anointing oil on his head, drawing the sign of the cross on his brow. Then the abbot raised up the new king and turned him to face the crowd of people, while two lords, one Dane and one Angle, came forward carrying between them a silver tray. On it, upon a red cloth, rested a marvelously worked arm-ring of gold, glinting with garnets and jet and bright winding patterns in the gold, like the ones in the pages of the Gospel book. The bishop took the arm ring, and the two men stepped aside while he held it up gleaming in the sunlight, crying, "He is worthy!" and placed the ring on Godfrith's arm.

The people cried, "He is worthy!" and "Hal, Guthfrith!" cheering until they were hoarse, while the new king looked out upon them, bowing his head to them over and over.

They heard a speech from him, but Edmund remembered it after as pictures in his mind—pictures of old folk sitting in peace around the hearthfire of a hall, thriving children laughing as they feasted on beautiful bread from a good harvest, churches rising from ashes, and even outlaws finding sanctuary from blood feud, with time to repent their deeds.

The day of celebration continued about the bonfires late into the night, but the bearers took Cuthbert back to the little church at Crec. "Well," said Stitheard to the three young laymen—Franco no longer being a novice—"We'll leave the monks to their prayers. You three can be off for the feasting and fun. Only mind you get no grease on those new tunics and cloaks!"

Franco ran off at once, while Edmund and Hunred were strolling out into the field where many of the visitors had camped. "What's his hurry?" asked Edmund.

"A girl," said Hunred.

Edmund drew up short. "What?" Had he misread Caris's eyes?

Hunred . . . smirked. "A milkmaid at Crec hall."

Edmund let out his breath. Then he looked at Hunred. "Is this *you* laughing at *me*?"

Hunred shrugged. The smirk was still there. "I think the race is over, Edmund. We've borne our saint on a long pilgrimage, but his new home is already being built at Cuncaceastre. You'd better go and settle things with Caris right now—or you know she'll go right after Franco again and steal him out from under that poor milkmaid's nose!"

Riddle flew out of the darkness to land on his shoulder and add his voice. "All right, I'm going!" Edmund laughed, and headed off toward the fires.

"Edmund!" Hunred called, and Edmund turned. Hunred strode up to him. "I used to think I wanted to be a saint. Now I don't know. But it's been good to bear the saint with you, Edmund." He held out his hands, and they clasped arms.

"And with you, brother," said Edmund.

✛ The End ✛

hiscorical noces

THE STORY OF THE WANDERINGS OF THE COMPANY OF Cuthbert with the body of their beloved saint comes to us largely in the *Libellus de Exordio* of Symeon of Durham. Symeon wrote more than two centuries after the events, but he asserts the account was passed on by the descendants of the original company. Still, Symeon had his particular bias as historians do, and also some details are unclear or disputed by scholars. An earlier document, the anonymous *Historia de Sancto Cuthberto*, says Cuthbert's body was translated from Lindesfarne to Norham some years before the Danish invasion of AD 875.

The *Libellus*, however, does not mention Norham when it says the bishop took "with him" the relics and "fled from the aforesaid island and deserted the church." As the Holy Island of Lindesfarne is so closely bound up with Saint Cuthbert and his devotees, it therefore seemed best to me for purposes of this fictional story to ignore the (possibly temporary) earlier translation to Norham, and begin the story with the company taking the saint's body with them from their home of Lindesfarne when they flee the Danes.

Symeon names only four of the seven coffin attendants: Hunred, Stitheard, Franco, and Edmund. All he says of them is that Hunred is the one who had the dream of the Gospel book's recovery and the horse being provided. Their characters and relationships in my book are otherwise entirely fictional, and I hope I have not offended against any of them for the sake of the story. The *Historia* gives us the names of some of their descendants, with a few anecdotes.

The king named Guthred or Guthfrith too is largely a mystery, though both the *Historia* and the *Libellus* tell of Eadred's vision commanding Guthred be made king. He is believed to be the same as one King Guthfrith, buried at York Minster in AD 895. I spell his name "Godfrith" in the book to show how the Anglo-Saxons might have pronounced his name differently from the Scandinavians.

Bishop Eardwulf, with the help of the visionary Eadred of Luel, led the company as I have portrayed him, as Symeon writes, "a man who always stood by Saint Cuthbert everywhere, in prosperity as well as in adversity."

The beautiful Gospel book that was washed overboard at Derwentmouth and later recovered is believed by some to be the famous Lindisfarne Gospels. Today they rest at the British Museum, but there is a popular movement to bring them back to the northeast of England, where they were created for the honor of God and of Saint Cuthbert.

Cuthbert's body was eventually moved one more time, from Chester-le-Street (Cuncaceastre) to Durham, where it rests today. In the museum in the cathedral crypt may be seen his wooden coffin, his famous jeweled cross, and some other relics.

Three literary items not from the *Libellus* or the *Historia* appear in this book:

First, the poem sung by the Danes at Cockermouth is *Havamal*, or "Sayings of the Wise." It is a form of ancient Scandinavian wisdom literature, parts of it much like the biblical Book of Proverbs, and connected with the god Odin. It is believed to date back at least to the ninth century. The translation is by W. H. Auden & P. B. Taylor.

An Old English poem too makes an appearance here, which Bishop Eardwulf in the story attributes to Cynewulf, the most famous Anglo-Saxon poet. However, no one is completely sure who Cynewulf was, when he lived, or whether indeed this poem, *The Dream of the Rood*, is really one of his. Parts of the poem appear on the seventh-century stone cross at Ruthwell. The translation in this book is my own.

Lastly, the story about Cuthbert and the ravens, performed by Aelfleda at Aelfsdene, comes from the *Life of Saint Cuthbert* written by the Venerable Bede. The verses she recites are from my own retelling of this story, which has recently been published in picture book form by Conciliar Press as *The Ravens of Farne*.

You can learn more about Saint Cuthbert, the Anglo-Saxons, and the Vikings at my blog, http://saintcuthbert.net

glossary

Latin words and expressions

CATHEDRA   The bishop's chair.

DEO GLORIA   Glory to God.

KYRIE ELEISON   This is actually Greek, not Latin, but it was used in the otherwise Latin services of the Western Church at this period. It means, "Lord, have mercy upon us."

MATINS   The church service sung at daybreak.

MISERERE   Have mercy.

NOCTURNES   The late-night prayer service.

ORA PRO NOBIS   Pray for us.

PRIME   The "first" hour, the church service sung in the first hour of daylight.

SCRIPTORIUM   The building where the monks write, copy, and decorate manuscripts.

TIERCE   The "third" hour, about 9 AM.

VESPERS   The evening service, at sundown.

Old English words and expressions

The language we call Old English was spoken in the island of Britain until after the Norman conquest (1066). It was the language of the Anglo-Saxons, who took the land from the prior inhabitants, the Britons, who were generally pushed to the north and west of the island. As in the English-speaking world today, there were different dialects in the different regions. The language of Northumbria, where this story takes place, has a modern descendant in the Tyneside dialect called Geordie, which may be the oldest form of the English language still in use.

Churl   A free common person.

Beoth gesund   Plural of "Waes thu hal" (see below).

Burn   A small stream. A term still used in parts of Britain today.

Danske tunga   The Danish tongue (language).

Furlong   The length of land an ox could plough in a day.

Lammas Day   "Loaf-Mass," the early wheat-harvest celebration on August 1, when new bread was brought to church for blessing. The barley harvest came a little later, depending on the local growing season.

Thegn   A nobleman, usually a warrior.

Mere   A lake.

Moor   A wide hill or hilly country.

Rod   A measure of around 16 feet.

Taefl   A board game of strategy.

Waes thu hal   Health to you, a general greeting like "hello."

Wealas   Wales or the Welsh, meaning "foreigners." It also at times had the meaning of "slave." The Anglo-Saxons took the east and center of the island of Britain from the Welsh, pushing them to the west and north, and took some of them captive to be slaves. Called Britons by the Romans, the Wealas called themselves the Cymraeg, or "fellow-countrymen."

WITHIES   Shoots of hazel or willow which sprout from the stump of a purposely cut tree. Used for building material.

Old Norse Words and Expressions

The invaders called "Danes" by the Northumbrians were actually from many different parts of Scandinavia, and they spoke several variants of the language we now call Old Norse. You may know of these invaders under the term "Viking." This is not a nationality, but means something like "adventurer." Many of the Old Norse words were close to Old English, and to a limited extent the Scandinavians and Anglo-Saxons would have understood each other.

FELL   Hill country. Replaced the Old English term *moor* in areas taken over by the Scandinavians.

HAVAMAL   "Sayings of the High One," an Old Norse poem presenting good advice and wisdom for young men. It is thought to originate around AD 800.

HRAFN   Raven.

HVERR FAR THAR NU?   Who goes there?

JARL   A chieftain or noble, equivalent in rank to an Anglo-Saxon thegn. From it comes the modern English term *earl*.

TARN   A lake. Replaced the Old English term *mere*.

places on the journey

NORTHUMBRIA was an Anglo-Saxon kingdom which, before the eighth- to ninth-century Scandinavian invasions, stretched across the "neck" of England from the north shore of the Humber River and into what is now southern Scotland.

For decades scholars have debated what the land looked like during the Anglo-Saxon period. Most agree that there was much more forest cover than there is today, but little detail can be determined with certainty about most places. Much of what can be guessed is based on the names of places. These names can change over time, sometimes to sound like they have a different meaning. In the story I have not been absolutely consistent about using Anglo-Saxon forms. Below I list some of the names mentioned in the book, not in alphabetical order, but in roughly the order the company travels to or speaks about the places.

LINDESFARNE, sometimes spelled Lindisfarne, now known as Holy Island, is today a place of pilgrimage for Christians, tourists, and history buffs, and for nature lovers who visit the nature reserve. For centuries visitors have arrived by walking barefoot across the sands at low tide; today you still must arrive at low tide, but you can drive across a causeway. The monastery was founded by Saint Aidan, and later Saint Cuthbert became abbot and bishop there.

Luel, now Carlisle in the Borders, was another of the many monastic houses in the diocese of Lindesfarne, and the home of Eadred the visionary.

Beblow Crag on Holy Island. *Crag* means what it means today, a rocky prominence; a castle was built there in the sixteenth century.

Bee-hall, perhaps the older form of the place name now shortened to Beal, may originally have meant the hall of a man named Bea.

Horton, Doddington, Shotton, Workington, Harrington. The *-ton* part of these kinds of names gives us our modern word "town" and means a settlement.

Mailros, now called Melrose (Scotland), is now the starting point of a long-distance walking path called Saint Cuthbert's Way, which ends at Holy Island. **Saint Cuthbert's Cave,** in the hills not far from the coast, can be reached via this path.

Gateham, a possible Anglo-Saxon form of **Yetholm.** The latter comes from the Old Norse, suggesting the Vikings settled at this place. The suffix *-ham,* like *-ton,* indicates a settlement, while *gate* may mean the entry way to the path over the hills, or it may mean "goat."

Langleeford possibly means "wide meadow by the river crossing-place."

GEDWEARDE, now Jedburgh (Scotland), had in the ninth century a church founded by one of Bishop Eardwulf's predecessors.

THE CHEVIOTS, the hills to the south of today's Scottish border. The name is of pre-Anglo-Saxon origin, but the tallest hill, shown on maps as "The Cheviot," is known locally as "Muckle" or "Great" Cheviot, from the Old English *mycel*. The long-distance path the Pennine Way goes north to south along the heights of this hill country (some of the loneliest in England), much of which today is within the bounds of Northumberland National Park.

AELFSDENE, now Elsdon. Probably the *-dene* or valley of a man named Aelf.

CROSSENSETTE, now called Corsenside. The name suggests there may have been a cross set up here. There are no remains, but such crosses are known all over the British Isles. They may have been used variously as boundary stones, rallying points, or educational aids.

HADRIAN'S WALL was built by the Romans long before the Anglo-Saxons came to Britain, and much of it is still standing today, even though some of its stones were removed for other building projects throughout history. The Romans also built many of the roads in Britain, including the DEVIL'S CAUSEWAY and DERE STREET.

WESTMORINGALAND, between modern Northumberland and Cumbria. In this region nearly all the hill country is referred to as *fells*, a Norse term, rather than by the Anglo-Saxon word *moor*. This shows that at some point the invaders took control of the area.

WORKINGTON is near **DERWENTMOUTH,** the mouth of the Derwent River, in present-day **CUMBRIA** in the northwest of England. The Lake District and coast of Cumbria hold some intriguing hints of ancient connections with Saint Cuthbert. **COCKERMOUTH** is the place where the Cocker River flows into the Derwent.

HWITERN or **WHITHORN** in Galloway, Scotland, also known as Candida Casa or the White House, is named for the monastery established there by Saint Ninian when he brought the Christian faith from Ireland to Britain, long before Saint Cuthbert's day.

OSWIESDUNE, where Guthfrith was made king, is today an unknown location; in the book I have placed it conveniently for the sake of the story not far from Crec. The *dune* or "don" part of the name means "hill." Oswy was an earlier Northumbrian king.

CREC or Crayke is the place where the company settled briefly after their long journey, until Eadred's vision commanding Guthred (Godfrith) be made king.

CUNCACEASTRE (Chester-le-Street after the Norman conquest) was the home for Cuthbert's relics for ninety years, after which they were brought to **DUNELM,** today's Durham. His body remains in the cathedral there today. Any place with a *-chester* in the name was once part of a Roman army camp.

EOFORWIC, modern-day York, was a bustling Saxon town until it was captured by the Scandinavian invaders in AD 867. They called it **JORVIK** and made it their capital and a major trade center, and it is now a major archeological site. York today boasts a famous Viking museum.

Whittingham is the name of the place associated with Guthfrith's youth.

author bio

DONNA FARLEY IS A WORD GUILD AWARD WINNER for Canadian Christian fiction. Her short stories have appeared in numerous anthologies and magazines in the US and Canada, including *Cicada* magazine for young adults. She has also published poetry and nonfiction, and is the author of the Conciliar Press book *Seasons of Grace: Reflections on the Orthodox Church Year.* Conciliar also recently published her first picture book, *The Ravens of Farne: A Tale of Saint Cuthbert.*

also by the author

The Ravens of Farne
A Tale of Saint Cuthbert
by Donna Farley, illustrated by Heather Hayward

The seventh-century Saint Cuthbert of Lindisfarne is one of England's most beloved saints, honored also by the Eastern Church. Saint Cuthbert's adventurous, yet humble spirit is demonstrated in this delightful tale of his encounter with an unruly raven.

The lyrical, humorous text and simple, charming illustrations of *The Ravens of Farne* will appeal to readers of all ages.

A picture book for children preschool age and up.

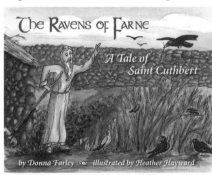

ISBN: 978-0-9822770-5-8
Format: paperback
Trim size: 9" X 6.75"
Page count: 32 pages
Price: $14.95
CP Order Number: 007650

To order this book or request a Conciliar Press catalog, please call Conciliar Press at (800) 967-7377 or (708) 587-4151, or log on to our website: www.conciliarpress.com.

Conciliar Media Ministries hopes you have enjoyed and benefited from this book. The proceeds from the sales of our books only partially cover the costs of operating our nonprofit ministry. We are committed to publishing high-quality books in a variety of formats with an Orthodox Christian worldview. Your financial support makes it possible to continue this ministry both in print and online. Donations are tax-deductible and can be made at www.conciliar-media.com.